W9-BOA-545

"Many years ago, Paul Hanly Furfey shocked my youthful complacency with his book, *The Respectable Murders*. His challenge helped set my life in a different direction. Now, decades later and his youthful vigor untempered by the treasure of years, he gives us *Love and the Urban Ghetto*. He chronicles a life-long pilgrimage through "scientific charity," "Christian personalism" and the Catholic Worker Movement, and now into exploration of liberation theology and democratic socialism. The challenge abides and Msgr. Furfey plows on—a relentless pioneer, a light on the mountain, a heroic witness from American Catholicism."

Joseph Holland, Center of Concern

PAUL HANLY FURFEY was born in Cambridge, Mass., in 1896. After graduating from Boston College, he entered the seminary of the Archdiocese of Baltimore, was ordained priest in 1922, and was assigned to the Catholic University of America. There he has served in the Department of Sociology for over forty years, and was Director of Social Research from 1959–1971. He also acted as Assistant Director of New York City's Research into Juvenile Delinquency from 1956 to 1961. In 1958 he received the papal medal *Pro Ecclesia et Pontifice* in recognition of his teaching, research, and writing, which includes over seventeen books in the field of sociology.

Love and the Urban Ghetto

Theodore Lownik Library
Illinois Benedictine College
Lisle, Illinois 60532

Love and the Urban Ghetto

Paul Hanly Furfey

ORBIS BOOKS

Maryknoll, New York 10545

The Catholic Foreign Mission Society of America (Maryknoll) recruits and trains people for overseas missionary service. Through Orbis Books Maryknoll aims to foster the international dialogue which is essential to mission. The books published, however, reflect the opinions of their authors and are not meant to represent the official position of the Society.

Library of Congress Cataloging in Publication Data

Furfey, Paul Hanly, 1896-
   Love and the urban ghetto.

   Includes bibliographical references.
   1. Liberation theology, 2. Church and the poor.
3. Sociology, Christian (Catholic) I. Title.
BT83.57.F87   261.8'34'41   77-16700
ISBN 0-88344-292-2

Copyright © 1978 by Orbis Books, Maryknoll, N.Y. 10545

All rights reserved

Printed in the United States of America

Contents

A Personal Preface

I grew up an Irish lad in Boston. To be such at the turn of the century was to be a member of a minority group. The WASPs were in control. They were the doctors, the judges, the mayors, the bank presidents, the intellectuals. The Irish were struggling upward from the level of pick-and-shovel men or housemaids. But we Irish had one big compensation. We were Catholics. On Judgment Day, the WASPs would be humiliated and we would be triumphant. Our loyalty to the church was intense.

As I saw it, our big responsibility on earth was to attain heaven; the best way to accomplish this would be to work at it as a full-time professional. I was completely convinced, from the earliest times I can remember, that my vocation was to be a priest. My parents, also, took this for granted.

Second, I very early developed a passion for social justice. Possibly the discrimination from which my Irish compeers suffered was the reason. I was sure that my vocation as a priest was not primarily a vocation for pastoral work among the people, attractive as that was. Rather, I was called to work for social justice, to promote Christian love on the group level.

And, third, I knew that I was called to be an intellectual. That was the way I was brought up. While I was a student in high school and college, my parents were pleased at any minor success I had in extra-curricular activities. But all such matters were, after all, secondary. The one essential thing was to do my very best in class. My studies always came first.

What was to be my next step when I was graduated from Boston College after eight years with the Jesuits? Should I join the order? The New England Jesuits in 1917 were very conservative and not scholarly—strange as this may sound today. If I joined them, I knew I would probably end up teaching Freshman trig or Junior logic.

But there was the Catholic University in Washington! In those days it was the only Catholic institution in the country with a comprehensive graduate program and with professors routinely doing research. So I won a Knights of Columbus scholarship, went to Washington, and soon found it was the place for me. After a semester, I went to the seminary

in Baltimore, joined the Baltimore Archdiocese, was ordained in 1922, and was assigned at
once to the university. I have been here ever
since.

At the university it was possible to carry out
my vocation as I had conceived it. I was a priest
and a social scientist devoted to the study of
social problems and to their solution. Intellectually, my career seems to have fallen into three
stages.

My first stage involved the scientific approach. I majored in sociology and later taught
in that field. In those days we used to talk about
"scientific charity." If we really love our needy
neighbors, we shall not be satisfied by trying to
help them in just any casual way. We must help
them as efficiently as possible. I embraced the
ideal of "scientific charity" with enthusiasm.

It seemed to me that the behavioral sciences
were the key to the solution of social problems.
We should diagnose and treat behavioral problems as we diagnose and treat physical disease.
If we can diagnose, we can treat and cure. It
gradually became clearer that physical factors
are important in the explanation of behavior. I
found, for example, very definite proof of the
effect of puberty on behavior. So I sought and

received permission to spend a year in Germany as a medical student.

That year in Germany was a turning point for me. In a way it was disillusioning. It turned out that there was little parallel between the medical and the behavioral sciences. Often at least, a physician can diagnose a definite ailment, prescribe a remedy, and cure the patient. However, that does not happen with juvenile delinquents. Their antisocial behavior does not have a single specific cause. Sometimes, of course, a delinquent may be reformed. But it is an uncertain process, not reducible to a straightforward scientific formula.

Something else happened to me in Germany, subtle and difficult to describe. As I became disillusioned with the purely scientific-empirical effort to understand human behavior, so at the same time I became more aware of certain super-empirical avenues to insight. During that winter in Berlin I went on a musical spree, spending evening after evening at the opera or at a symphony concert. Face to face with mystical beauty, I realized ever more clearly that there are other roads to a deep understanding of human behavior, roads that do not lead through the psychological or the statistical laboratory.

Then I also had some technical reasons for disillusionment. The tests that researchers used in studying human behavior were rather amateurish. Then, too, the mathematical methods they used to analyze test results were often quite unsound. I expressed my disillusionment in a number of articles in technical journals.

A second stage began for me when I visited the Catholic Worker house in New York in 1934. Dorothy Day and Peter Maurin had an answer to social problems: Take the New Testament literally. Love your neighbors as yourself and treat them on that basis. Peter and Dorothy welcomed homeless dispirited men and women from the Lower East Side and treated them as close personal friends sharing with them their food, their shelter, their clothing. In those cramped and dingy quarters on East Fifteenth Street I discovered an intense spiritual beauty.

Some of my colleagues in the Sociology Department at the university became interested in this new spirit of Catholic social activism and decided to experiment. Dr. Gladys Sellew founded Il Poverello House and Dr. Mary Elizabeth Walsh founded Fides House, both in the heart of the Washington black ghetto. They saw the ghetto people in a wider perspective. We began to do sociological studies on the entire subject of ghetto life.

In many ways life at Il Poverello House and at Fides House was a beautiful experience. It was an experiment in interracial living, something most unusual in those days. Moreover, it was a beautiful experiment in practical Christian charity. And it was sociologically illuminating. However, after more than two decades, we realized that it was not the complete and final answer to the problem of poverty. That problem arises from the very nature of our economic system. The system is such that, even in times of relative prosperity, millions of people remain unemployed and that fact makes poverty inevitable. Something had to be done about the economic system itself.

Later I heard about the development of liberation theology in Latin America and a third stage in my thinking opened. The liberation theologians were very conscious of "social sin." Economic injustice is sinful in just as true a sense as individual sin. The existence of poverty in the midst of affluence is just as nasty and disgusting as sodomy. Christians must be concerned with building a just society just as earnestly as they are concerned with making individual persons holy. In 1974 I went to Latin America to see the activities of liberation theologians at first hand, and I returned convinced. We must be revolutionists in the sense that we must advocate fundamental socio-economic change. We must reject the current form of capitalism. This follows from any real understanding of New Testament teaching. Of course the application of liberation theology to the United States will require a great deal of thought and cautious experiment.

When I look back on my intellectual work of half a century, it sometimes seems that I have spread myself rather thinly over a very wide area. Am I perhaps a jack-of-all-trades and a master of none? But when I think deeply, it seems to me that my intellectual life has been a sort of pilgrimage. I ranged widely, but I gradually gained deeper insight, more understanding of the ills of our society.

I began with a rather naive faith in "scientific charity." Yet my early research in child psychology and problem families gave me many valid insights. It is helpful if one comes to realize even slightly how the world looks through the eyes of a feeble-minded child. Life in a broken, disunited family is a very special sort of experience. It is worth while to spend effort in trying to understand what that experience means to an individual. In Germany for a year I rubbed shoulders with people whose cultural background was very different from my own. That was illuminating. Yet it was no less illuminating when I began to understand something about the cultural differences between ghetto life and middle-class life. The Catholic Worker group did not have all the answers; yet their life was inspirational. Down in the Bowery and later during travels in Europe I learned something enormously important from people who tried to take the New Testament literally. In Latin America, liberation theology is still only in process of development. Those theologians do not yet have all the answers by any means. Yet they have given me a most valuable new perspective.

So perhaps, after all, it was not a mistake to spread myself so thin, to try to cover so many fields. Perhaps it was the necessary road to insight.

Whatever insight I have achieved, I here share with you.

PAUL HANLY FURFEY

Chapter One

Love Is Everything

The twenty-fifth chapter of St. Matthew's Gospel presents a surprising picture of the Last Judgment, surprising, that is to say, in the light of our common Christian concepts. The passage is enormously important for Christian social thought.

How We Shall Be Judged

In that chapter Christ states very clearly and explicitly that a person's eternal fate will depend on the performance or nonperformance of the corporal works of mercy. Those who helped the needy will be saved; those who did not will be damned. Nothing is said about the other virtues and vices. Apparently no one is rewarded for a life of chastity or for fervor in prayer or for heroic penance. No one is condemned for murder or robbery or blasphemy or adultery.

The texts are quite explicit. "Come, O blessed of my Father, inherit the kingdom prepared for you from the foundation of the world; for I was hungry and you gave me food, I was thirsty and you gave me drink, I was a stranger and you welcomed me, I was naked and you clothed me, I was sick and you visited me, I was in prison and you came to me" (Matt. 25:34–36). Not a word more about the virtues of the virtuous. They helped their neighbors in need. That was enough. No other qualification for heaven is mentioned.

On the other hand, there is the judgment of the damned: "Depart from me, you cursed, into the eternal fire prepared for the devil and his angels; for I was hungry and you gave me no food, I was thirsty and you gave me no drink, I was a stranger and you did not welcome me, naked and you did not clothe me, sick and in prison and you did not visit me" (Matt. 25: 41–43). Again, the corporal works of mercy are the criteria and the only criteria.

But this account of the Last Judgment is really not surprising. For one who practices the corporal works of mercy in a genuinely Christian manner must necessarily practice all the other Christian virtues as well. St. Paul is very explicit about this: "He who loves his neighbor has fulfilled the law. The commandments, 'You shall not commit adultery, You shall not kill, You shall not steal, You shall not covet,' and any other commandment are summed up in this sentence, 'You shall love your neighbor as yourself ' " (Rom. 13: 8–9).

Charity is traditionally defined as a supernatural virtue by which we love God above all things for his own sake, and our neighbor and ourselves for the love of God. Charity is a single virtue; it is indivisible. Whoever, then, love their neighbors with this special sort of love must also love God and must love themselves too with the unselfish love of charity. Such love obviously excludes sin; for we do not offend those we love.

The saved merit heaven by loving other human beings. "Truly, I say to you, as you did it to one of the least of these my brethren, you did it to me" (Matt. 25:40). This is the whole moral doctrine of the New Testament. There is one way, and only one way, to achieve salvation. That is to practice the virtue of charity, to help our needy neighbors. That is the whole story.

Our Current Christian Morality Is Different

The central importance of charity does not seem to be clearly recognized by today's average Christians. Our current moral concepts depart rather clearly from the principles of the twenty-fifth chapter of St. Matthew in ways presently to be discussed. The fault is with ourselves. We tend to be sloppy in our thinking. We do not squarely face the radical teachings of the New Testament. We overlook one statement; we misinterpret another; we fail to draw some obvious conclusion from a third. And thus we fashion for ourselves a comfortable morality that is clearly different from that of Christ and the apostles.

To begin with, our morality tends to be negative. The sole condition for salvation is the avoidance of serious sin: It is, of course, praiseworthy to practice virtues, to receive Holy Communion daily, to be active members of pious societies, to do volunteer work in a Catholic hospital or settlement house; but the one really essential thing is to avoid serious sin. That will be the one point on which our eternal destiny will be decided at the Last Judgment.

This negative attitude, this emphasis on the avoidance of sin rather than on the practice of virtue, is probably the basis on which most of us examine our conscience. As children we were taught in catechism class a specific list of sins to be avoided. We were taught to examine our consciences before confession by reading through such a list of sins prepared for this purpose and printed in the prayer book. "Have I been guilty of backbiting, slander, calumny, rash judgments? Have I taken pleasure in bad thoughts? Have I failed to pay my just debts?" And so on and on and on.

So the standard way we assess our spiritual status is to ask ourselves about sins committed, not about virtues practiced. This is a very different principle from that revealed in the account of the Last Judgment, where the sole criterion was the practice of charity and sin was not mentioned.

Traditional moral theology is infinitely more sophisticated than the old grade-school catechism. Yet the general approach is surprisingly similar. The emphasis, almost the entire emphasis, is on sins to be avoided, rather than on virtues to be practiced. There are long discussions of specific sins with learned references to the authorities. And the dividing line between mortal sins and venial sins is treated at length. Precisely how much money must one steal to deserve hell? Can the amount be reduced to dollars and cents? People may steal so-and-so many dollars, die unrepentant, and eventually attain heaven. But if they had stolen just a bit more, eternal punishment would await them.

It is only fair to add that recent moral theology has been rapidly moving away from such narrow assessments of the seriousness of specific sins. More attention is being given to the sinner's intention, to his state of mind, to the circumstances of the act. Yet in spite of these rather radical changes, it seems not unfair to state that our moral theology is still principally sin-oriented. It is still essentially negative.

This negative point of view leads to absurdity. It is nonsense to say that the fewer sins people commit, the holier they necessarily are. If this were the case, idiots would be the holiest persons in the world; for they cannot distinguish right from wrong, lacking as they do what is called "the use of reason." Even the great saints committed some sins. What made them holy was not the absence of sin, but the presence of heroic virtues, all summed up in the great virtue of charity, Christian love. Naturally this great love excluded all but the most minor sins. However, this was a secondary effect; they avoided sin because they loved.

Bourgeois Morality

This salient characteristic of our everyday morality, its negative character, is also characteristic of the current socio-economic elite, successful businesspeople and their various allies. They tend to be selfish and ruthlessly competitive, but they avoid the standard sins. They avoid outright deception in business. They do not openly steal. They control their tempers. They keep out of sensational sex scandals. They are often or usually good church members. In a word, they avoid the sins that are bad for business. Obviously, if the economic system is to proceed smoothly, there must be a certain amount of mutual confidence, an absence of violent disturbance, a certain smoothness in interhuman relationships.

There is a close similarity between this bourgeois morality and the common negative Christian morality that has been mentioned. There is nothing in this negative morality to offend ambitious businesspeople and their allies. In fact, there seems to be a rather cozy relationship between the church and the business world. A bishop is likely to choose his official residence in a fashionable neighborhood where his neighbors are members of the business elite. The bishop may develop close friendships with these people and choose them as members of the various boards of directors of Catholic institutions. They become trustees of Catholic colleges. The students and the faculties of these colleges look up to them. The courses offered, and the courses that the students demand, are adapted to the preparation of students themselves to become members of the business elite.

Certainly this bourgeois lifestyle, which seems to be sanctioned by our current negative morality, was not the lifestyle exemplified by Jesus Christ. There is no reason to believe that the Holy Family at Nazareth lacked the basic necessities, the food, clothing, and shelter necessary for a normal life. On the other hand, it is very clear that they had little beyond these basic necessities. The life of working people in those days was simple. It yielded the minimum necessary income, but only at the cost of unremitting, hard work. Such was the lifestyle Jesus deliberately chose for himself.

If Jesus taught poverty by his example, he taught it also explicitly in his words. The classic passage is Matt. 19:16–26. He told the rich young man, "If you would be perfect, go, sell what you possess and give to the poor, and you will have treasure in heaven; and come, follow me." Voluntary poverty is essential to perfection; but Christ's teaching went beyond that. "Truly, I say to you, it will be hard for a rich man to enter the kingdom of heaven. Again, I tell you, it is easier for a camel to go through the eye of a needle than for a rich man to enter the kingdom of God." When the disciples were shocked at this statement, he added, "With man this is impossible, but with God all things are possible." In other words, it requires a miracle of grace for a rich person to be saved. Not a very comforting thought for the millionaire!

The New Testament is insistent on the danger of riches; this point is so little emphasized among Christians today that it deserves further discussion. First, it is important to ask precisely what the word "rich" means in the New Testament. Since the economy of the first century was so different from ours, it is not safe to assume that the word meant then precisely what it means now.

Once I studied all the persons spoken of as "rich" in the New Testament.[1] What sort of persons were they? How did they gain their wealth? These persons fell into three separate classes. First, there were the landowners.

These might run huge farms, a class probably typified by those mentioned in James 5:4 who unjustly withheld the wages of their farm-hands. Or they might rent out their land to tenant farmers, like the man in Luke 20:9 who "planted a vineyard and let it out to tenants." Another class of the rich were merchants engaged in interregional trade. Rev. 18:2–3 mentions Babylon (which symbolizes Rome) and the fact that "the merchants of the earth have grown rich with the wealth of her wantonness." It is interesting, by the way, to read in Rev. 18:11–13 a list of the typical wares that these merchants traded. A third class of the rich may be called financiers. They dealt directly with cash. They contracted for the right to collect certain customs duties or tolls. Zacchaeus was one of these. Then there were the bankers. Here doubtless belong the moneychangers whom Christ ejected from the Temple. This was a traditional activity of bankers, as was also the lending of money at interest (mentioned in Matt. 25:27).

It is very important to note that all these various classes of rich mentioned in the New Testament have one quality in common. They were all actively engaged in the pursuit of gain. No one is condemned for the mere possession of money. In our own day people are called "rich" if they possess wealth, no matter whether it came to them through inheritance or by their own active efforts. The latter is what the New Testament condemns. 1 Tim. 6:10 states that "the love of money is the root of all evils." Not money as such, but the *love* of money, is what corrupts. A real passion for wealth tends to monopolize a person's energy. Little is left for the service of God. "No man can serve two masters. . . . You cannot serve God and mammon" (Matt. 6:24).

It is interesting to note that the classical Greco-Roman authors give an equally unflattering account of the acquisitive rich. Such people loved money passionately. They had an exaggerated idea of their own importance. They lived lives of luxurious self-indulgence. Even when they gave their money away, they did not always do so intelligently and constructively. There is a grim inscription at Minturnae in Italy that boasts to posterity that the deceased had once sponsored a gladiatorial show in which no less than eleven first-class gladiators were slaughtered. There were indeed rich people who were mentioned with respect by the classical authors; however, they were not the acquisitive rich, but those, like Pliny the Younger, whose wealth was inherited.

The foregoing explains an apparent paradox. In spite of the condemnation of the rich in the New Testament, the church has canonized some very wealthy persons. St. Louis of France is a good example. Being king, he controlled the state treasury of his country, yet personally he lived a very simple life and used the money he controlled to promote the welfare of his people. He possessed money, but he did not love money. He was not acquisitive. So, too, with the other wealthy saints. They were not tainted in the slightest degree by that *love* of money that is the root of all evils.

It is important also to understand what is meant by "poverty" in the Christian tradition. Sometimes the word means penury, a lack of sufficient funds to buy the basic necessities. In this sense poverty is an evil. The saved in the twenty-fifth chapter of Matthew are rewarded because they did what they could to alleviate this sort of poverty by performing the corporal works of mercy. On the other hand, the voluntary poverty practiced by so many saints, or the poverty of the Holy Family, means an absence of luxury, a contentment with merely enough money to permit a normal existence and the performance of the duties of one's state of life.

Bourgeois Morality and the Poverty Problem

The present book deals with the poverty problem, more particularly as it exists in the black ghettos of our American cities such as Washington. Those Christians who adhere to the bourgeois, negative moral code discussed above will surely do little toward solving the problem. For their code does not include the overwhelming obligation of sharing whatever one has with those in need.

It is distressing to reflect how little emphasis this obligation receives in our educational institutions, in Sunday sermons, in the religious press. The corporal works of mercy are indeed discussed and praised. But they are praised as though they were merely good works in excess of our moral obligations, as "works of supererogation," as the technical phrase has it. How seldom is it made clear that charity, expressed by such works, is our central moral duty, the duty that spells the difference between heaven and hell!

Once this point is grasped, a further difficulty remains. Precisely how are individual Christians to help their neighbors in need? In some instances, the answer is not difficult. A man who has money that he and his family do not actually need may know some relative, some neighbor, perhaps a former employee, who stands in need of help. Here the obligation is clear. But what about the vast numbers of the poor in our city slums? They constitute the real poverty problem.

Middle-class people with money to spare may of course give to certain charities that aid specific groups among the poor. They may give to some home for dependent children or an institution for the aged poor or a denominational hospital. They may contribute to a charities drive that aids a broad spectrum of such institutions. This, beyond a doubt, is praiseworthy. Yet the important fact remains that the vast areas of poverty that exist here in the United States continue to exist in spite of such giving, and will continue to exist even if such giving is vastly increased. Some other way must be found. What that way is forms the central topic of this book.

Chapter Two

Social Sin

In order to treat the problem mentioned at the end of the last chapter, it is necessary to define and discuss "social sin," a concept much emphasized by the liberation theologians of Latin America.

The Nature of Social Sin

The common sins, such as those discussed in religion classes, are committed by an individual or by an agreeing group of individuals. This person told a lie. That person took the name of God in vain. These three, acting together, robbed a bank. Once the facts are known, the sinner or sinners can be clearly identified. Even when criminals are legally insane and are morally and legally not responsible, they are nevertheless identifiable as the personal cause of the evil act.

But not all sins are like this. Consider the existing poverty in the United States, for example. It is clear that no one individual or group of individuals decided to create this poverty and can therefore be held responsible for it. Indeed, even the most selfish capitalists must be unhappy about this poverty. If there were no poor, they would not have to pay taxes to support the welfare system. If there were no poor, more people could afford to buy more consumer goods, and profits would be higher. Poverty is bad for business.

Poverty is the fault of the economic system, the very way the community is organized. It is a social sin, not the sin of an individual. A great many social problems are the result of social sin. Indeed, whenever a problem can be identified, social sin must be suspected as being at least one factor in its causation.

Even in some cases where individuals would seem to be wholly responsible for some injustice, social sin can be discovered as at least a contributing factor. It is a notorious fact that in this wealthy country itinerant farmworkers are usually grossly underpaid and otherwise unfairly treated. Here the individual farm owners would seem to be clearly responsible. Yet, if one owner should decide to raise wages more than slightly, that owner would also have to raise the price of the product. Then that owner would lose out in competition with other farmers and go out of business. It would seem that farmers as a group, rather than the individual farmer, are responsible for the injustice. Of course the individual farmer who refuses to join in fair and just collective bargaining is personally responsible. Unfortunately there are too many such farmers today. However, the fact remains that the unjust treatment of farm workers is an example, at least partially, of social sin.

Slavery in the United States would seem to be a very clear example of an evil due to the sins of individuals. The slave owner, the slave trader, the politician who defended slavery, appear to be examples of persons who committed grave social injustices for their own selfish purposes. This would seem clear; yet here is a surprising fact that needs to be taken into account: Many persons of unquestionably high character participated in the system. George Washington, and many others among the Founding Fathers, held slaves. So did the great Archbishop Carroll. So did religious communities, including Jesuits, Capuchins, Dominicans, along with Ursuline and Carmelite nuns. Unbelievable as it may seem, it is probably fair to assume that such people failed to understand how overwhelmingly evil the system was. Such is the power of unified public opinion. So it seems plausible that slave holders like these, although objectively guilty of very serious sin, were nevertheless subjectively guiltless. Slavery was an enormous social sin. It was evil because it deprived the slaves of elementary human rights; but it was evil also because it so flagrantly distorted the consciences of so many decent people.

If the individual citizens are not responsible for social sin, are they not at least responsible for doing what they can to remedy it? Most certainly they are. Specifically, to cite the problem discussed in this book, they must do something to alleviate the poverty around them. But what? They can, of course, share their money with some needy friend or neighbor whom they know. They can give to organized charitable agencies. Yet such generosity does not attack the root causes of poverty itself. What these root causes are and how they might be attacked will be discussed later. Here, however, one point needs to be stressed as strongly as possible. Individual Christians have a very grave obligation to do what they can. The description of the Last Judgment shows clearly that one's reaction to this obligation makes the difference between heaven and hell.

It will be helpful at this point to review the Christian reaction to the poverty problem in the past. What was the policy of church leadership? What did individual Christians of heroic virtue do about the poor? Like the liberation theologians, perhaps we can glean some principles from the study of Christian history.

Christian Tradition and the Problem of Poverty

The New Testament introduced a fresh concept of social responsibility. Christ spoke of his precept that his disciples should love one another "even as I have loved you" as "a new commandment" (John 13:34). It was a break with tradition. "You have heard that it was said, 'You shall love your neighbor and hate your enemy.' But I say to you, Love your enemies and pray for those who persecute you" (Matt. 5:43–44). Individual Christians must do everything they can for those who need help, no matter who they are.

Before considering how the early Christians put this command into effect, one must bear in mind one very important fact. The Roman Empire in those days was a totalitarian government. The emperor had dictatorial power. It would have been completely useless, then, for Christians to try to force the unjust socioeconomic system to change.

What the Christians could do, and actually

did, was to try to abolish poverty in their own community. "Now the company of those who believed were of one heart and soul, and no one said that any of the things which he possessed was his own, but they had everything in common. . . . There was not a needy person among them, for as many as were possessors of lands or houses sold them, and brought the proceeds of what was sold and laid it at the apostles' feet; and distribution was made to each as any had need" (Acts 4:32, 34–35). The process of distributing available wealth and helping those in need was a complicated task. Therefore special persons—the deacons—were appointed to take charge (Acts 6:1–6). This mutual giving was not confined to individual communities. Paul took up a collection in the churches he founded for the poor in Jerusalem. He had quite a bit to say about this; see particularly 2 Cor. 8:1–9.

The early Christians did not directly attack the Roman socio-economic system. However, they did have influence. They broke with the current mores and adopted a striking lifestyle of their own. They did not attack the Roman government publicly, but this lifestyle of theirs was visible and it impressed their neighbors. Tertullian reported that the pagans used to remark, "See how these Christians love one another." The Christian way of living was a tacit rebuke to the pagan way. Their example was a silent sermon in favor of a different sort of life. Eventually Christianity won out and became the predominant philosophy of life. The change was very gradual; but the Edict of Milan, in A.D. 313, may be considered the turning point.

The transition from paganism to Christianity brought about a change in official attitude toward poverty and the poor. The history of governmental and voluntary agencies for poverty relief is long and complex. Throughout the Christian era the nature of the prevalent poverty itself shifted with changing economic conditions and therefore different approaches to its relief were called for. The detailed story of the Christian reaction to the poverty problem throughout the ages is far too complex to be discussed in detail here. However, three important aspects of the Christian praxis do deserve mention.

The first is the insistence on personal poverty, that is, the renunciation of personal wealth beyond what is necessary to live in health and decency and to perform the duties of one's vocation. Wealthy Christians have been

encouraged to sell their possessions and give to
the poor. Of course kings and rulers could not
do this because their wealth was not a personal
possession but an adjunct to their office. But it
was their duty to live simply and to use this
wealth not for personal pleasure, but for the
benefit of their subjects.

It is easy to see why one cannot spend one's
riches on selfish luxury and still love one's
neighbor as oneself, a love absolutely fundamental to the Christian ethic. For the total of
human wealth is limited; and if one has more to
spend, someone else must have less. To enjoy
luxurious living while a neighbor lives in want
is clearly the negation of Christian morality. So
the rich must share with the poor.

Jesus himself lived in poverty, not in actual
penury, but at the modest level that represents
the New Testament ideal. To be a good Christian is, by definition, to imitate Christ, and this
means by definition to renounce all that is
superfluous. This ideal has been institutionalized in the religious life. One of the three
essential religious vows is the vow of poverty.
There have been abuses of course, but over the
ages the religious life has meant the renunciation of the possibility of becoming rich. Thus
the religious life has represented a sharp and

definite break with the popular equation of wealth and success.

A second effect of the traditional Christian attitude is the recognition that the oppression of the poor is a serious moral evil. In other words, poverty amid affluence is a social sin. Throughout history Christians have lived under widely varying economic systems; and the particular form that oppression of the poor has taken has varied from system to system. Here it is sufficient to remark that Christian moralists have always been conscious that economic systems, like other human activities, are subject to the moral law.

To point out the existence of economic injustice does not, of course, automatically solve the problem. For the forms of economic injustice here discussed are social sins, evils, that is to say, of society rather than of the individual. Consider usury as an example. It is not enough to reform an individual usurer; for others will continue the evil as long as usury itself is permitted. Social sin demands social action. A conscientious government, for example, may promulgate a law against usury. Over the centuries Christian thinkers have had an influence in promoting this type of constructive public policy.

A third aspect of the relation between Christianity and poverty is the constant recognition that the corporal works of mercy are an absolutely essential element of Christian morality. Helping the poor has a long and glorious history within the church. It was St. Ambrose who said, "The possessions of the church are the patrimony of the poor." During the Middle Ages, one of the principal concerns of the monasteries was giving alms to the needy. More recently, a number of religious communities have been founded with the principal objective of performing the works of mercy or perhaps some specialized work, such as caring for abandoned children or the aged poor. Then there have been very active lay societies, for example, the Ladies of Charity or the Society of St. Vincent de Paul. In addition many lay persons have distinguished themselves by their own person-to-person generosity.

Christian charity has been characterized not only by the amount, but also by the spirit of this giving. Modern social work emphasizes the importance of detachment. Caseworkers must not become emotionally involved with their "clients." They must retain their objectivity so that they may assess the facts clearly. This is a very different attitude from that of the saints who met the poor with a warm, personal love, treating them as dear friends, as indeed they were.[1]

The saints felt that the poor deserved the very best. St. Conrad Birndorfer (1818–94) was for many years the doorkeeper at the Capuchin convent at Altötting in Bavaria. As such, it was his duty to respond to the beggars who knocked on the convent door. For this purpose he insisted on the best food from the convent kitchen, the best beer from the brewery, and the best vegetables from the garden. Sometimes he would complain to the cook and the brewmaster that they were getting careless and the food and beer were not good enough for the poor.

St. Madeleine Sophie Barat (1779–1865) founded the Society of the Sacred Heart and became superior. One day at her convent the nun in charge of the linen room complained that the best chemises were being given to the poor. These, she felt, were too good for them. St. Madeleine was shocked. "Too good!" she exclaimed, "Too good for the poor! Why, my child, I would give them my skin if I could."

The lesson is clear. It is, after all, the lesson

of the twenty-fifth chapter of Matthew. Our salvation depends on our generosity to the needy. Moreover, and most remarkably, Christ has identified himself with the poor.

No Room for Compromise

It is not difficult to be generous with the poor as long as we place what seems like a "reasonable" limit on this generosity. Thus a rich man may surround himself with all sorts of creature comforts and yet give large amounts of money to charitable causes. It would seem possible to enjoy the best of two worlds, to enjoy the prestige and the comforts of worldly success and at the same time be a model Christian by giving very generously to the poor.

This double standard is widely followed and widely approved. We have only to read the biographies of some prominent and widely respected Christians. So-and-so was born a poor boy, but by indefatigable and intelligent effort he built up a large business and became a millionaire, indeed, a multimillionaire. But he was also an outstanding Christian. He served very actively on the board of the local charities. He built and partly endowed a home for the aged. And so on. When he dies, the bishop presides at the funeral and speaks his praise of the man as a model Christian.

All this is very familiar; yet it is also very false. Nothing in the New Testament, nothing in the tradition of Christian holiness suggests that one may be devoted to the pursuit of gain and to a holy service to the needy at the same time. Indeed, the lesson is the precise opposite. "No man can serve two masters. . . . You cannot serve God and mammon" (Matt. 6:24). That is precisely what the rich philanthropist is attempting. His ultimate loyalty must be to one objective or the other. He cannot move in two different directions at once.

In this connection the life story of St. Mary Micaela Desmaisières, Viscountess of Jorbalán, is instructive. She was born in Madrid, January 1, 1809. Her family was rich, not in the New Testament sense of being actively acquisitive, but in the sense of having plenty of money. The family was also socially prominent. Therefore it was possible for the growing girl to lead a very active social life. It was a constant round of balls and parties, and she enjoyed every moment of it. After the death of her mother in 1841, she spent time in Paris and in Brussels where her brother held important positions in the diplomatic service. In these cities, too, her happy social life continued to her intense delight.

There was, however, another side to the life of the viscountess. She was intensely devoted to the works of mercy. She interested herself in the education of young girls. She cared for the sick poor, visiting them in their homes. For a time she ran a sort of informal hospital in her palace where she lived. In 1834 during a great cholera epidemic she was heroic, risking her own life in caring for the sick.

Thus it seemed that the viscountess had combined two contradictories, in spite of New Testament teaching. At the same time she thoroughly enjoyed her wealth and showed by her works an intense love of the poor. In 1845, however, something happened that eventually created tensions between her two worlds. While back in Madrid on a visit, a friend took her to see a hospital, and she was deeply moved at the plight of the delinquent girls she found there. She realized how desperately they needed help. So she opened a house as a refuge for such girls, put someone in charge, and then returned to Paris, and later to Brussels.

On a visit to Madrid in 1848 she found that the house she had started was in a bad way. She turned it over to a group of French nuns; they, too, proved unsuccessful. There seemed to be only one remaining alternative. The viscountess herself had to move in and take charge. She did so, others joined her, and the group began to live as an informal religious community. She did not find this life easy. When the group decided to wear habits, for example, the viscountess had a skilled dressmaker fit her with a silk habit. The others wore wool. Reluctantly, however, she realized the absurdity of such compromises. Gradually the great lady renounced her privileges and learned to perform cheerfully the humblest tasks. Her sacrifice became complete. Appropriately enough, when she died on August 24, 1865, she died at Valencia as a martyr to charity. She went there to nurse cholera patients and succumbed to the disease.

So there seems to be no compromise between the Christian code and conventional worldly success. To be a good Christian, one must be a failure by worldly standards. This sounds foolish. Is it actually the New Testament standard? If so, is not the standard itself foolish?

Christian Foolishness?

Paul admitted that the New Testament standard was indeed foolish to worldly eyes. "For the word of the cross is foolishness to those who

are perishing" (1 Cor. 1:18). And those who
preached the gospel had to be "fools for Christ's
sake" (1 Cor. 4:10). They lacked the distinction
that would impress an educated audience.
They could not pose as intellectuals. "Where is
the wise man? Where is the scribe? Where is the
master of worldly argument?" (1 Cor. 1:20).

To the pagan sages of the first century,
Christianity seemed to be a fad, an aberration
popular among the uneducated or among those
who were not quite sane. They looked on it as
we look on astrology or palmistry or witchcraft
or numerology. It was a belief that lacked intellectual respectability. *Of course* Christianity is
foolishness.

Paul realized that all this was part of the
divine plan. God had endowed human beings
with intelligence. Through our natural wisdom, we should have come to know God and
thus to realize our moral obligations both toward God and toward others. But, by and
large, we failed to accomplish this. So the Al-
mighty offered another, and different, opportunity. We must come to a knowledge of the
truth by way of faith, and this faith must be
strong enough to accept even that which appears foolish to human wisdom.

Has not God made foolish the wisdom of the world?

For since, in the wisdom of God, the world did not know God through wisdom, it pleased God through the foolishness of what we preach to save those who believe. For Jews demand signs and Greeks seek wisdom, but we preach Christ crucified, a stumbling-block to Jews and foolishness to Gentiles, but to those who are called, both Jews and Greeks, Christ the power of God and the wisdom of God. For the foolishness of God is wiser than men, and the weakness of God is stronger than men (1 Cor. 1:20–25).

During the first centuries, to be a Christian was to defy worldly prudence. It meant taking one's life in one's hands. Persecution was sporadic, and in many places Christians enjoyed long periods of peace, but persecution could be unleashed at any moment. A new emperor, or even a new local administrator, might bring a sudden change of policy and the Christians might have to choose between martyrdom and the abjuration of the faith. Under such circumstances few would be willing to accept baptism casually. Being a Christian was serious business.

In this country in our own day we do not suffer religious persecution. We can feel certain that we shall not have to choose between renouncing the faith or dying a cruel death. However, we do have to make another choice, much less dramatic, but no less real. We have to choose between two standards of conduct. There is the worldly standard that equates success with the acquisition of wealth. People look up to the person of means. On the other hand, the Christian standard frankly demands voluntary poverty, that is, the renunciation of wealth. And it demands, too, an active concern for the needy.

Chapter Three

Poverty Is Death

Granted that Christians have a most serious duty to relieve poverty, the next logical question concerns the nature and extent of this poverty; for the problem cannot be met intelligently unless it is first understood.

Worldwide Poverty

Some four billion people are alive in the world today. A shocking proportion of them are too poor to afford an adequate diet. We often hear calculations like the following: Every day twelve thousand people die of hunger; ten million children the world over are so seriously malnourished that their lives are in jeopardy; last year a billion people suffered from hunger and malnutrition.

Unfortunately it is impossible to prove or disprove such statements with scientific rigor. Much of the existing hunger and starvation occur in countries where the nature of illnesses and the causes of death are neither carefully determined nor systematically recorded. The only statements that can be made with assurance are rather vague ones. But it would seem safe to say that some hundreds of millions suffer from dietary deficiency diseases that make normal life impossible for them and that perhaps twice as many are malnourished to the extent that they cannot reach their full human potential and are more likely than others to die from communicable disease.

Somewhat better information is available on average per capita income and average life expectancy for inhabitants of various countries. Figures show that people in poor countries have shockingly brief lives. Such data are published regularly by the U.S. Department of State. It should be noted that "per capita income" is here defined as either Gross National Product or Gross Domestic Product divided by the country's population. It is important to note that this is not equivalent to average wage. Department of State figures for four particularly disadvantaged African countries are as follows: For Chad, per capita income, $73, life expectancy, 43 years; for Guinea, $80 and 33 years; for Mali, $81 and 38 years; for Togo, $134 and 40 years.[1] In contrast, figures for the United States for the same period give per capita income as $7101 and life expectancy as 71.9 years.

It is tempting to be proud of this country's long life expectancy. It appears to reflect a very high quality of health care. One must, however, make one important exception to this generalization. The poor receive low-quality care in this affluent land. A recent study points out that "at least 15 nations have a longer life expectancy at birth than the United States" and then goes on to point out the reason for this: "The relatively high mortality of the United States compared with other advanced nations is undoubtedly in large measure a reflection of the high mortality of the disadvantaged in the nation—the lower socioeconomic groups of whites and the even more disadvantaged minority groups."[2]

It is understandable that people in the poorer countries die young. It is not excusable but it is understandable. For it is clear that potential for agriculture varies enormously from country to country, that some countries are not able to feed their population out of existing resources, and that many such countries do not have the cash available to buy food abroad. Clearly, some efficient system for international food sharing needs to be worked out. Such a system does not now exist. As long as it does not exist, widespread hunger and low life expectancies seem inevitable.

It is harder to understand why widespread poverty should exist in this affluent country. It is conventional to boast that this is a land of opportunity, that a poor person with courage and ambition can become well-to-do, that no one able and willing to work need suffer poverty, and that even those unable to work are adequately cared for through social insurance and the welfare system. Alas, this rosy picture is far from true. Numerous studies show that many Americans are caught in a hopeless poverty from which they are unable to extricate themselves, and numerous other studies show that the poor die young. The present book deals specifically with poverty in the United States and, more particularly, with poverty in the urban ghetto and its tragic results.

Hunger and Poverty in the United States

In this country there are over 25 million poor people. Of course the number varies from year to year. At the present writing the latest census estimate applies to the year 1975. The figure was 25,880,000.

By census definition, to be poor means to be undernourished. This follows from the way the definition was worked out. First, the National Research Council published estimates of the minimum essential elements of nutrition needed by both sexes and at various ages. Then home economists from the Department of Agriculture translated these standards into concrete diets, some more expensive, some less expensive. The cheapest of these diets was not recommended for routine use; it was only for "temporary or emergency use when funds are low." Then all these various diets were priced at food stores. Thus it was possible, given a person's age and sex, to specify the cheapest adequate diet for such a person. The next step was to define "poverty." Various studies had shown that low-income families tend to spend about one-third of their total income on food, and two-thirds on shelter, clothing, medical care, and the other necessities. So the cost of the cheapest diet was multiplied by three to yield a cut-off point for poverty. It was assumed that people with less than this income would lack the cheapest possible necessary diet and would be equally badly off with regard to the other necessities of life.

The census publishes poverty cut-off standards for families of various composition. These figures are periodically revised to allow for changes in the cost of living. In 1975, the year of the poverty figures quoted above, the figure was $5,500 for a non-farm family of two parents and two children.

The census definition of poverty has some obvious defects. First of all, it is based only on cash income including, of course, welfare payments. It does not take into account such things as free school lunches, food stamps, free meals for the aged, or gifts of food and clothing from persons who feel obliged to help an indigent relative. The census makes only one attempt to allow for non-monetary income. A lower cut-off point is set for farm families than for non-farm families, on the assumption that farm families can obtain some of the needed food from the farm itself.

On the other hand, the diet on which the poverty standard is based rests on two rather gratuitous assumptions. One is that a needy family will have the facilities and the know-how to put the economy diet on the table. This implies a good deal of shopping and cooking skill. It implies access to food stores with reasonable prices. It implies that the buyer has enough money at hand to buy in quantity and save. It implies the availability of good refrigeration, a good stove, and good cooking equipment. One needs little familiarity with slum conditions to realize how unrealistic such assumptions are.

Again, living on the minimum economy diet demands a certain heroism. If the boy in the family spends a few cents for a Coke and some potato chips like his companions, he has already broken the diet. If the father buys a six-pack of beer for the weekend, he too has failed. If the mother pays the baker a dollar for a tiny cake to celebrate her daughter's birthday, that is one more forbidden excess. Old and young must stick to a rigorous, unappetizing diet, day after day, week after week, or they will be malnourished.

A statement from the Campaign for Human Development of the U.S. Catholic Conference takes sharp issue with the government standard. It estimates that the actual number of those who realistically should be called poor is "at least" 40 million. It brands the official yardstick as "radically unfair."

All the poor, by definition, have an income too low to buy the cheapest possible diet that will barely avoid malnutrition. To be just a bit below the minimum is to be malnourished.

However, not all the poor are lucky enough to be "just a bit" below. Hard statistics are lacking; however, from the shape of the income curve it seems reasonable to estimate that half the poor have no more than two-thirds of the standard income that defines poverty. In other words, many of the poor are *very* poor. Their diet is not merely insufficient; it is grossly insufficient.

The Poor Die Young

It is not hard to understand why poverty should be associated with early death. To begin with, the poor are malnourished. Malnutrition takes various forms. It may be a simple lack of food, too few calories. Or the diet may be unbalanced. For example, protein deficiency is common and serious among the poor. A good diet implies the presence of a number of vitamins and minerals and of course some of these may be absent. Malnutrition is a complicated medical subject. Yet in all its forms it damages health and makes the patient more liable to contract diseases.

Many other concomitants of poverty also threaten health. Overcrowding is associated with poverty. This can interfere with sufficient rest. Moreover, it helps the spread of communicable disease. A poor man with a bad cold cannot have a room to himself.

The poor are likely to have bad housing. Insufficient lighting, loose floorboards, broken furniture may cause accidents. Accidents are also common in homes where a mother must work during the day and cannot give her young children proper supervision. In old houses peeling paint containing lead may be eaten by young children with tragic results. Where there is not enough play space in yards and neighborhood playgrounds, children must play in the street in spite of the traffic dangers.

Good health demands proper clothing. Without it one cannot be properly protected against rain and cold. Inefficient washing facilities interfere with personal hygiene. Dirty clothing and lack of personal cleanliness facilitate the spread of disease.

"Medical services based on extant biomedical knowledge are not being adequately delivered to the disadvantaged in the United States."[3] It is true that both free clinics and Medicaid can bring expert service to the poor. However, it is certain that on the average this service is less expert and less readily available among the lower classes.

Moreover, good health is not preserved solely by expert medical service. Often poor people cannot afford to carry out the doctor's orders. An obvious example is malnutrition. Suppose a doctor prescribes precisely the best diet for a malnourished person. If the patient is poor, this does not help much; for poverty makes an adequate diet impossible anyway. The situation is still worse when some special diet is called for, as in a case of diabetes. Such a diet, of course, costs more than an ordinary adequate diet. The patient who is unable to afford the latter is still less able to afford the former. Or suppose that a construction laborer has a heart attack from which he recovers satisfactorily. The physician tells him he is lucky, but that of course he must avoid hard labor in the future. What can the man do? His only salable skill is precisely the sort of hard work that can be fatal for him. Yet he is not technically unemployable. He is merely unemployable at the only sort of work he understands. The poor cannot afford good health.

Poverty is correlated with poor education. Here is another health hazard. An educated man can discuss his case with the physician more intelligently. Probably he has read a little about health care and knows more about per-

Theodore Lownik Library
Illinois Benedictine College
Lisle, Illinois 60532

sonal hygiene than the less educated. The poor
are likely to consult physicians less frequently,
usually only when symptoms have become
alarming. Routine physical examinations are
important, but less common for the poor. Also
the poor are more likely to have superstitions
that affect health and to rely on home remedies.
Good health care requires intelligent cooperation between patient and health personnel and
this cooperation is harder for the uneducated.

A good many studies have shown a correlation between good health and various other
factors. Those in the professional and manage-
rial occupations are healthier than those otherwise employed and the differences are most
striking when they are compared with unskilled laborers. The higher the income, the
lower the mortality. Whites outlive nonwhites.
Good education is good for health. And so on.

All these studies are interesting and they are
valuable as far as they go. But they do not fully
account for the tragic mortality in the ghetto.
The point is that in the ghetto these various
hazards not only combine, but they also in-
teract. It is true, for example, that blacks have a
higher mortality rate than whites. This is not
necessarily true of middle-class blacks, but it is
horribly true of ghetto blacks. In general, the

lower the income, the higher the death rate. Yet some segments of the low-income population are normally healthy. College students, for example, may have to practice extreme economy until they graduate and get a good job. But low income is life-long in the ghetto. Moreover, as will be discussed later, the ghetto has a distinctive lifestyle; it is a way of life that can in itself be unhygienic.

To realize fully the life-destroying quality of life in the black urban ghetto, it is not enough to consider isolated elements of ghetto life. We must consider it as a whole and contrast it with middle-class life as a whole. It must be considered concretely. Therefore a particular section of the Washington black ghetto will now be described in detail.

Service Area 6, Sub-Area B

For statistical purposes the District of Columbia is divided into nine "Service Areas," and each of these is subdivided into three to five "Sub-Areas." The campus of Catholic University is located in Service Area 2; so its characteristics are quite familiar to the writer. It is by no means a fashionable quarter. Rather, it is quite ordinary, 84.5 percent black, with a median family income, in 1970, of $12,141. There is little poverty, but no real hint of luxury. The area has a standard mortality ratio of 73. This means that its age-adjusted death rate is 73 percent of the death rate of the District of Columbia as a whole.

Now consider a smaller quarter that may be thought of as the heart of the Washington black ghetto, Service Area 6, Sub-Area B. This is almost totally black, 98.3 percent, and the median family income is $5409. However, the absolutely startling and tragic characteristic of Service Area 6, Sub-Area B is its standard mortality ratio. This is 212, three times that of Service Area 2.

The contrast is not between the rich and the poor. It is between the middle class, perhaps the lower middle class, and the ghetto poor. It is a contrast between a predominantly black area of modest income and an area in the very heart of the black ghetto. The area is more than merely poor. It is tragically neglected. It is neglected by health personnel, by the educational establishment, by recreational leaders. The extent of this neglect is dramatized by those horrible death rates. Every year about 300 people die in Service Area 6, Sub-Area B. If the death rate there were the same as in

Service Area 2, only about 100 would die. Because we force them to live under such appalling conditions, an extra 200 die annually. They die undramatically. We do not flaunt our cruelty. Yet they are just as dead as those who died in Hitler's ovens.

Service Area 6, Sub-Area B is the heart of the Washington black ghetto. Here the ghetto lifestyle is found in its most extreme degree. This chapter and the following one will describe life in this particular district. However, one should bear in mind that the lifestyle described is also found, though usually in a less extreme form, in much larger areas of the city.

Some of us in the Department of Sociology at the Catholic University have had a strong interest in the Washington ghetto, an interest that has extended over decades. Much of our personal research and much of the dissertation research of our students has been focused on this area. In February 1936, Dr. Gladys Sellew of the Department bought a house in the area, which she named Il Poverello House. She moved in and began a project there. Being a trained nurse, she was particularly interested in the health problems. Another member of the Department, Dr. Mary Elizabeth Walsh, lived in the ghetto from 1938 to 1958 and founded a neighborhood center which she called Fides House. Both these houses were interracially staffed, many of the staff being graduate students from the University.

From 1965 to 1971, I was project director of a large research project financed by the National Institute of Mental Health: the Infant Education Research Project. As the name implies, it was primarily concerned with the mental development of infants; but it included a most intensive study of the whole family environment of twenty-eight children from the age of fifteen months until after they entered school. All these families lived in the ghetto area. The study was very thorough; to finance it, NIMH spent $470,887 through the University's Bureau of Social Research, plus additional funds spent directly through the Institute's own personnel.

The Lifestyle of the Washington Ghetto

Before our findings on the ghetto lifestyle are discussed, it is appropriate to say something about the word "ghetto" itself and its relevance in this connection. The word literally refers to the walled-in districts of some European cities in which Jews were compelled to live in past

centuries. Lower-class blacks are of course not
legally confined to certain sections of Washington; but they are confined there by social pressure and by economics. It is not easy for a
family to move out of the Washington ghetto.
Landlords do not welcome them elsewhere and
they would feel out of place. The term "ghetto"
is also appropriate for another reason. In the old
European ghettos the Jews developed a society
of their own with its own characteristic lifestyle; blacks have done something similar in the
Washington ghetto.

In Service Area 6, Sub-Area B, 37.1 percent
of persons were at or below the poverty line at
the time of the latest available statistics. As
remarked before, many of these were not
merely poor, but very poor. They were *far*
below the poverty line. One should remember
also the criticism given above of the census
definition itself. Doubtless a great many not
poor by this definition were actually living in
great want. Also, the economic status of ghetto
families is very variable. A family not poor this
year may have been poor last year. It seems safe
to assert, therefore, that nearly all ghetto
dwellers have been handicapped, some more,
some less, by very real poverty.

As previously stated, malnutrition is implied

by the census definition itself of poverty. Malnutrition was a constant finding of our ghetto studies. Sufficient food was often lacking. Poor stoves, poor refrigeration, and lack of adequate kitchen equipment made food preparation difficult. Mothers often lacked cooking skill. Working mothers often lacked time. Not infrequently, the gas or electricity was turned off. The IERP staff reported that lack of money affected the type of food as well as its quantity. Diets tended to be high in carbohydrates and lacking in vegetables. There was little red meat except in hamburgers. Meals were often served irregularly.

The results of such conditions were various. Sometimes there was chronic hunger. It is hard for middle-class people to imagine what this means. All of us have missed a meal now and then by some mischance and we know how unpleasant this can be. But chronic hunger is something else, something quite different.

Once a member of the IERP staff, on a visit to one of the families, found a preschool boy down on his hands and knees picking up bread crumbs from the filthy floor and avidly stuffing them into his mouth.

Once at Il Poverello House we celebrated the birthday of a staff member by giving her a dinner there. Of course it was a simple dinner, pork chops, because we did not want to eat anything more expensive in a poverty neighborhood. After the dishes had been washed we went into the front room to socialize a bit. One of the staff members had to go back to the kitchen. She returned to report that a little neighborhood girl had been picking through the garbage can near the kitchen door. She had found a pork chop with a little meat still remaining on it and she was hungrily gnawing at it. That is the sort of hunger that you and I do not understand.

Even when ghetto dwellers are able to afford enough food to avoid actual hunger, they are often unable to afford the right kind of food. Middle-class people with a reasonably adequate food budget tend to select a fairly balanced diet, although they too make mistakes. But a bad diet is often forced on the poor. So, even if the diet has enough calories, it may be otherwise insufficient, most often, probably, by lack of sufficient protein.

Malnutrition leads to lethargy. Once Western Union of Washington decided to hire more messengers from black areas. So several boys from the Fides House neighborhood were hired and provided with shiny new bicycles. They were delighted. However, their delight was temporary. They simply lacked the physical energy to pedal a bicycle all day long. Sometimes middle-class people accuse the poor of being lazy. Who wouldn't be lazy if they didn't have enough to eat?

The worst effect of inadequate food is not just hunger or languor. It is death. Malnutrition lowers resistance to disease. Remember that statistic about the death rate in the midghetto being three times that of a normal area.

It was stated above that in general poverty implies poor housing. Our own studies found this to be very true in the Washington ghetto. Falling plaster was common. There were broken holes in ceilings and walls. Dr. Walsh tells of one woman whose bedroom ceiling leaked whenever it rained. The landlord was kind enough to have the leak repaired—after five years of urging. Statistics show that overcrowding is common for the Washington poor and this was only too evident to our staff. Lack of suitable furniture was another feature. IERP staff reports contain items like these: "Old, broken-down furniture . . . No tables; sat on floor to write . . . Extremely dark; one small lamp . . . No floor covering . . . No mattresses; just bedsprings . . . Not enough beds to go around."

Rats, mice, roaches, bedbugs, all sorts of vermin were common. Of course these pests were unpleasant, but they were also bearers of disease. There were several cases of young children being bitten by rats. There is not much that an individual family can do to control vermin, for the vermin infest entire blocks, rather than individual homes. If one dwelling is cleared of rats, others invade from adjacent houses.

Such conditions encourage the spread of communicable disease. When Service Area 6, Sub-Area B is compared with the more normal Service Area 2, death rates for influenza and pneumonia are found to be 3.29 times as high in the former. Disease rates for syphilis are 6.24 times as high; for gonorrhea, 3.34 times as high. Perhaps the most significant fact of all is this: Rates for newly reported active tuberculosis are 8.54 times as high in Service Area 6, Sub-Area B.

The IERP staff found home accidents to be common. The total death rate from accidents is 2.78 times as high in Service Area 6, Sub-Area B as in Service Area 2.

What was said above about the medical care of the poor in general was also confirmed by our studies. At the time our research was in progress such care was almost always provided by clinics and hospitals rather than by private physicians who might be reimbursed by Medicaid. We are not competent to evaluate the quality of such care, but certain difficulties were evident. The clerical personnel at the clinics were often impolite. On the other hand, doctors and nurses were courteous, but they spoke a technical language that was not understood. In this connection it is interesting to recall one Fides House program that consisted of regular meetings at which a physician merely answered questions about the meaning of medical terms: "They said I had diabetes. Is that serious?" "What is a thrombosis?" "Is a 'cerebral accident' the same as a 'stroke'?"

Service at clinics is said to be free for the poor. But this statement must be accepted with reservations. A mother takes a day off from work to take her sick child to a clinic. She pays the clinic nothing, but she loses a day's wages. Certain services are offered only at particular clinics which may be a long way from the patient's home. So there is at least a round-trip bus fare to be paid; or if there is no covenient bus route and if the patient is weak, even a taxi may be necessary.

Preventive medicine is rare in the ghetto. Children very often are not immunized against common childhood diseases until such immunization is required on entering school. Consequently preschoolers are often unnecessarily ill. Adults did not have regular physical examinations. They seldom went to clinics until the condition became serious. Home remedies were often used when middle-class people would have gone to a physician. The following IERP report is typical: "Boy swallowed a bottle of aspirin and ate Ex-Lax. Mother treated him herself. Did not go to doctor. Kept him awake and gave him lots of liquids. Mother very calm. Staff member urged her to go to the clinic, but she would not."

All in all, the staff impression of health care in the ghetto was very discouraging. Health care is expensive if it is to be effective. The poor cannot afford this. They cannot afford to live.

And So . . . ?

Here in Washington in Service Area 2 the median family income was $12,141 at the time of the last census. In Service Area 6, Sub-Area

B it was $5,409. The difference is $6,732. The death rate was three times as high in the latter area as in the former.

There is a direct relationship between the lack of that $6,732 and the trebled death rate. It is not hard to understand why people die young in Chad or Guinea or Mali or Togo. These are poor countries. But the United States of America?

A lady sits in an elite jewelry shop on Connecticut Avenue. She is fingering a necklace. Should she buy it? It is a bargain at $7,000; but, after all, she could easily afford something better. A man is talking to his real estate agent. He can easily afford the $200,000 asked for this new house. But he hesitates. He is considering a better house at $300,000. He would not really be taking much of a chance if he signed up for the more expensive place. A woman visits a fashionable boutique to select next season's wardrobe. The price will run to four figures. But of course she can afford it.

In this country we spend $2,500,000,000 for commercial pet foods each year. That figure divided by $6,732 equals about 371,361. So if we spent that money in the ghettos, we could raise the standard of living of some 371,361 families to a level of decency where the death rate would be lowered by two-thirds. But of course it is foolish to talk of such a policy change. We want the very best for those adorable puppies and kittens. As for those black kids in the ghetto—let them die.

Chapter Four

Poverty Is Despair

To live in the ghetto is to face physical suffering—hunger, pain, sickness, and then early death. Yet this is not the whole story. Ghetto life involves mental anguish that may be even worse. This is hard to describe and understand because it is internal, psychological. It cannot be documented simply by objective facts, as a high mortality rate can be documented. Yet, to understand ghetto life realistically, this inner torment must be taken into account.

Ghetto Dwellers Disdained

To be accounted a success in our society, one must usually be financially comfortable. People gossip enviously about the luxurious life of the wealthy. Probably the most common ambition among young people planning their lives is to become more or less like these successful people.

Of course one may attain fame and distinction in other ways. One may become a famous artist, writer, musician, a well-known stage personality, an inventor or a great scientist. However, success in these vocations is not independent of money. Who is a great artist? The one whose paintings sell. Who is a great inventor? The one whose invention sells. Of course some great writers have lived and died in poverty. However, at some time after their death their works began to sell widely. That is when people began to realize their greatness.

Success in politics, the attainment of high public office, is another criterion of success. Here too, however, money enters in. High office brings high income. And those in high office show a surprising love of this high income. Spiro Agnew fell because love of money corrupted him. He failed to become president because he accepted unethical gifts. And the most surprising fact was that these gifts were only thousands of dollars, not millions. His love of money must have been simply overpowering.

Money seems to tempt even good and sincere people. Catholic religious take a vow of poverty and nearly all are rather faithful to it. It should seem obvious that such an attitude is a necessary consequence of taking the New Testament seriously. Yet many prominent churchmen buy expensive mansions for themselves and live in some luxury. Lay people, too, who are publicly praised as model Christians, often spend a good deal of money on personal comfort and display. It seems as though Christian thinking, some sectors of it at least, reflects the common notion that success means monetary success.

Consequently, it is no surprise that ghetto dwellers rank so low in public esteem. For, if success means money, they are outstanding failures. A man who can barely support his family is not a success. However, people give him a grudging respect for his independence. Somehow or other he manages to make out and he and his family lead a more or less normal life. But the welfare family! Here is the ultimate disgrace. Here is the exact antithesis of success. The welfare family must simply forfeit our respect. And most ghetto dwellers whom we studied, if they were not on welfare at the moment, lived very near the welfare level.

Why Are They Poor?

It is very easy to make the mental jump from the proposition that ghetto dwellers live around the poverty level to the proposition that they so live through their own fault. However, before agreeing with the latter proposition, one startling fact should be taken into account: Poverty is an integral and inevitable feature of our U.S. economy.

At the present writing almost 8 percent of the U.S. work force is unemployed. This is admittedly higher than usual. People hope that the figure can soon be reduced to 5 percent or even less; but it would be thoroughly unrealistic to hope that it would go down to zero. In considering these figures, we should remember that they take into account only the jobless who are actively seeking work. There are many others who would like to work, but have given up the search as hopeless. Unemployment figures do not take these into account.

Of course not all who are unemployed at a given time are actually poor. Some are temporarily supported by unemployment compensation or by union funds. Some lose one job, but quickly find another. However, a large proportion of the jobless are chronically unemployed and a great many of these are ghetto dwellers. Chronic unemployment is a necessary consequence of the fact that there are just not enough jobs to go around. When someone from the ghetto does get a job, it is likely to be low paid, to involve tiring physical labor, to offer little or no hope for advancement, and perhaps to be temporary.

Granted that a substantial amount of unemployment is inevitable in our economy, and granted therefore that some must lose out in the competition for jobs, why is it that some persons rather than others are the losers? To narrow the question a bit, why is it that people from the black ghetto are so regularly among the losers? Is the fact not due perhaps to some defect either of ability or of character? Perhaps ghetto dwellers are simply born losers.

There is no reason to believe that ghetto dwellers are either stupid or shiftless. There are other valid reasons. First of all, dwellers in the black ghetto are black and this is in itself a handicap. Not that there is any reason to believe that blacks are mentally inferior. Admittedly this statement is a controversial one. The literature on the point is enormous and highly technical and it cannot possibly be summarized in the space here available. So let the following statement stand by itself: It has never been scientifically proved either that whites are superior to blacks in native intelligence or that blacks are superior to whites.

What is clear beyond a doubt is that blacks are sociologically handicapped. The era of out-right discrimination in hiring is now happily ending. Both legislation and a shift in public opinion are responsible for this. Yet it would be unrealistic to argue that skin color plays no part at all in current hiring practices. What seems to have superseded outright prejudice between the races is a certain feeling of strangeness. Whites and blacks are not quite at ease with each other. Having a black working side-by-side with a white involves a certain psychological adjustment. Educated blacks and whites learn to get along; but the case of ghetto blacks is different.

Ghetto blacks have a lifestyle which, to others, seems strange in many ways. Probably the most distinctive feature of their lifestyle is their dialect. They do not speak the same sort of English as educated Americans, either black or white. They even speak differently from un-educated whites. Many mistakenly think of ghetto speech as simply "bad English," or they believe that ghetto people "make mistakes" when they talk. These views are now known to

be false. There is now an extensive literature on
the distinctive speech of black Americans.
Their special dialect is called by linguists
"Nonstandard Negro English" (NNE). The
special language of the Washington ghetto has
been carefully studied by two of the present
writer's students.[1]

NNE has a long and involved history. Its
origin can be traced back to the days of the West
African slave trade. The captured slaves spoke
a large number of different African languages.
So a common language was worked out that
both the slaves and their captors used. This
language was a compromise that involved a
vocabulary that was almost entirely English,
but a grammar and a pronunciation that were
widely influenced by African languages. Such
a compromise language is technically called a
"pidgin" language. NNE, including the
Washington ghetto dialect, has descended from
this pidgin and retains some of its features.
Putnam and O'Hern found this to be true in
their Washington study. The vocabulary was
found to be almost entirely Standard English,
but its grammar and its pronunciation were
quite distinctive.

To try to describe the pronunciation used in

the Washington ghetto would be very technical. However, this attempt is not really necessary. Most of us have at least a rough idea of how spoken NNE sounds and how different it is from Standard English. Differences in grammar are very interesting. Thus the conjugation of verbs is different and expresses different shades of meaning. Putnam and O'Hern reported phrases like "I give her the present last week," where the past tense has the same form as the present. More interesting still is what linguists have called "invariant be." Thus "He sick" means that the person referred to is sick just now, whereas "He be sick" implies that the illness is chronic. Invariant be is used to express a continuous condition.

Differences like those given do not imply that ghetto English is inferior to Standard English. The meaning of "I give her the present last week" is just as clear as the conventional "I gave her the present last week." And "He be sick" or "He sick" both actually tell us more than the usual "He is sick." Ghetto English is different from our Standard English, but the differences no more imply inferiority than do the differences between French and English.

Although ghetto English is not in itself inferior, it can be socially and economically disastrous. The reason for this was brought out clearly by an experiment that was part of the Putnam-O'Hern study. Twelve black subjects were selected, representing a wide spectrum of social status. They ranged from university professors, a bookkeeper, a stenographer, skilled workmen, to the wife of an irregularly employed construction worker who lived precariously in the slums. To each of the twelve a short fable was read and they were asked to repeat it in their own words. These responses were recorded on tape and were presented in a random order to seventy judges, including both sexes and both races. The judges were asked to express judgment of the speaker's social status on a rating scale. The results were amazing. There was a correlation of .80 between these ratings and an objective measure of social status. So one can judge people's social status by hearing them speak just a few sentences. This can be done with no other clues at all, without knowing anything about the speaker's appearance, place of residence, occupation, income.

It does not take much imagination to guess the social implications of this. Low social status, betrayed by language, disqualifies one for a white-collar job. An applicant may be well qualified by intelligence, appearance, training, and ability. But what businessman wants to hire a receptionist who says, "He be sick"?

Another reason why ghetto residents can so seldom rise above the poverty level is the influence of the general lifestyle of the area. Consider a middle-class boy whose father is at least reasonably successful in his business or profession. His family, his friends, his neighbors, expect him to become a middle-class adult and to carry on the family tradition of success. Almost surely he will graduate from college. Perhaps family connections will help him to a desirable job. Pressure to succeed in a middle-class sense is subtle, but it is constant and very strong. Of course girls are also subject to this same sort of influence.

The life of ghetto children is very different indeed. Their parents are poor, undereducated, and very often separated. They know that they cannot attend college. They find the curriculum at local public schools uninteresting and poorly adapted to their needs. Like their own parents, other adults in the neighborhood are unemployed, underemployed, or employed at low-quality jobs. The odor of failure is all around them. It is not surprising if their lives are shaped by the neighborhood tradition, that they live and die near the poverty level.

Unsatisfying Work and the Failure of Family Life

The fact that the jobs of ghetto dwellers are so poorly paid and so irregular imposes an economic burden. Poverty is cruel. But there is also a psychological burden involved in such jobs. A certain feeling of accomplishment is essential to mental health. It is easy to understand the triumphal satisfaction of a great artist, scholar, inventor, social reformer. It is obviously satisfactory to know that one has made a contribution as a doctor, lawyer, teacher, or as a police officer, mail carrier, or fire fighter. In fact, most white-collar jobs and most skilled-labor jobs bring a sense of satisfaction. One has a sense of belonging. By attaining certain skills, by working conscientiously, these people attain a sense of self-satisfaction, a feeling of belonging, a consciousness of playing a needed role in society.

It is different in the ghetto. The unskilled jobs available there are likely to be menial and laborious. Whatever people may say about "the dignity of labor," they still think of dishwashers, cleaning women, and day laborers with little respect, if not with outright contempt. This common opinion spreads to ghetto workers themselves. It is hard to be proud of one's job if the rest of society despises it. So the ghetto worker goes to work without pride, without interest, without enthusiasm.

Ghetto jobs are humiliating because they have no future. A college student is not ashamed to work part time as a dishwasher or a cleaning woman, for the job is of course only temporary. After college, the student will get a better job, one with a future. But ten years from now the ghetto dishwasher will merely be a more experienced dishwasher.

It is hard to be proud of a job that requires no skill. Perhaps a good many white-collar workers do not appreciate the skill of an expert carpenter. But the carpenters themselves are conscious of it, and so are their fellow workers. They all know that it takes years of training and experience to attain such skill. But what is there about a busboy's work to be proud of?

And so the ghetto workers face their future with gloom. For them the future holds no promise. Elliot Liebow, who studied a group of Washington ghetto men, has this to say about the ghetto worker's view of his future: "It is a future in which everything is uncertain except the ultimate destruction of his hopes and the eventual realization of his fears."

There are indeed some families in which

home life is pleasant in spite of the fact that the wage earner's income is low and the job uninteresting. However, a certain minimum income is necessary to make even this sort of home life possible, and many or most ghetto families have incomes below this minimum. It is therefore not surprising that broken homes are common. A recent census report states that, among black families with incomes under $4,000 in 1974, less than a fifth of the children had both parents in the home. In the one-parent families the parent present was the mother in an overwhelming proportion of the cases.

Our own studies reflect the same conditions. At one time, when the IERP study focused on the point, it was found that only the mother was present in 16 of the 28 families. Remember that this study included only families with a young child present. Doubtless there would later be more separations. There was also a good deal of flux in family make-up. A husband and wife might break up, reunite, and then break up again. So, even in the two-parent families, separation might be a threat. In many ghetto families the man and woman had never been legally married. Such consensual unions, as they are called, are even less stable than the others.

It is significant that in nearly all the one-parent families, it was the man who was missing. A man feels a strong urge to play the masculine role. In our society this usually implies marrying, having children, and being either the recognized head of the family or at least a major participant in family decisions. To live like this is to be a man. But in the ghetto, as Liebow well says, the man "enters the job market with the smell of failure all around him. Jobs are only intermittently available. They are always menial, sometimes hard, and never pay enough to support a family."

The psychological effect of all this on a man is devastating. Instead of finding strength and happiness in family life, he finds failure. Not seldom he tries to compensate for his feelings of inferiority by beating his wife. This may give him, irrationally of course, a feeling of masculine superiority; but it dramatically worsens family life. In other cases the man turns to alcohol. Drinking further drains the family budget and the alcoholic is at a further disadvantage in the job market.

So ghetto families frequently break up. The man may simply disappear, or the wife may assert herself and drive him out. In any case, the woman is left in a difficult position. If there are only one or two children, she may arrange day care for them, get a job, and manage to survive. When there are more children, this is not practical. Usually the only alternative is to apply for welfare, in this case, Aid to Families with Dependent Children. This is not a happy solution. AFDC is notoriously insufficient to support a family normally. During the IERP study it was found at one point that the eight mothers receiving AFDC had total family incomes ranging from 56 percent to 77 percent of the poverty cut-off point. So, even after the welfare payments, these families were in deep poverty. Yet the District of Columbia ranks rather well in size of AFDC payments. Government statistics show that payments per recipient are higher here than in about seven-tenths of the states and territories. Apparently it is government policy to let welfare families live in poverty with the suffering and health hazards that this involves, but not to let them die of outright starvation.

Crime and Delinquency

It is a familiar fact that both juvenile delinquency and adult crime are high in slum areas. This is true of the Washington ghetto. Service Area 6, Sub-Area B has, by the latest figures, a juvenile delinquency rate of 60 per 1000, by far the city's highest and 2.79 times the rate for the city as a whole. Adult crime rates for the area are not available. Undoubtedly they are also very high; for crime and delinquency correlate.

A first impression from these figures might be that ghetto people are lawless. However, two facts ought to be taken into consideration in this connection. First of all, to say that the delinquency rate for an area is 60 per 1000 is to say that 94 per cent of the youths in the area were not accused of delinquency during a year. Remember, too, that the delinquency rate is based on referrals to the juvenile court. By no means were all the youths referred found to be delinquent. It is clear, then, that a great many of the young people in the city's worst delinquency area are law-abiding.

Moreover, when all categories of offenses are taken into account, probably ghetto people are not guilty of more offenses than middle-class people. However, offenses in different social classes are of different types. A well-known sociologist, Edwin H. Sutherland, has coined the term "white-collar crime" for the sort of crime committed by persons of high social status. This includes, for example, restraint of trade, misrepresentation in advertising, infringement of patents, financial fraud. Those accused of such crimes are seldom brought into court for trial as criminals; still less often are they sent to prison. Sutherland's viewpoint has become still easier to accept in these post-Watergate days. We are beginning to realize how common bribery is. Think, for example, of the huge bribes paid by multinational corporations, such as Lockheed, to officials of foreign governments in return for contracts. We have learned that even high government officials will approve outright burglary when it suits their purposes.

Probably few realize that the poor despise the rich as immoral just as much as the rich despise the poor. People in the ghetto see many injustices against themselves. Landlords are remiss in making required repairs. Merchants pressure ghetto people to buy luxuries that they cannot afford, and the prices for these luxuries are exorbitant. The poor work for low wages under tough conditions without unions to press for justice. In the eyes of ghetto people, police do not stand for equal justice under law. Rather, they are seen as the arm of the middle and upper classes, enforcing the law selectively.

The frequency of violent crime in the ghetto is one more fact that makes life there so difficult to endure. It is a constant physical and financial hazard. Statistics show that most victims of lower-class crime are themselves lower-class people. One young man from the Fides House neighborhood was shot and killed in a gambling dispute. Another killed his wife, his father-in-law, and then himself. A boy from an IERP family was murdered on his way home one evening. There were other serious crimes and many minor ones against these people. White-collar people often complain that the streets of Washington are unsafe at night. If this is true for them, it is even more true for ghetto dwellers.

Then street crime is a constant temptation in the ghetto. If a family cannot balance its budget, for example, the father may think of robbery as a solution. Of course middle-class fathers are tempted also. However, they are likely to think of some chicanery, some shoddy deal, which may cause trouble for them, but is less likely than a violent crime to lead to a prison sentence.

In the long run, perhaps the most serious effect of ghetto crime is the divisiveness it creates in our society. It furnishes a certain rationalization for class antagonism. Middle-class people feel less obligation to help the poor when they tell themselves that such people are immoral and do not deserve help. In those comparatively rare cases when ghetto people directly attack the well-to-do, crime may be a subtle form of revenge. There must be a special thrill in robbing a prosperous-looking man at gunpoint. For the moment the robber has the power of life and death over him. In the case of a woman he can add the threat of rape.

Outcasts

The most significant characteristic of ghetto dwellers, probably, is their isolation. A man is not likely to get a conventional job and join a union. Of course he is even less likely to go into business for himself. He is neither a capitalist nor a proletarian. He is outside the economic system. Also, since he finds himself unable to maintain a stable family life, he is outside the system of blood relationships that binds people into familial groups. This isolation is psychologically devastating.

Nor is a woman better off. Her role of mother is restricted by the fact that she must probably work outside the home to support her children or else live miserably on AFDC. She, too, does not belong.

Exposed to such conditions, some break down completely, turn to alcohol, and sleep in vacant buildings. Others face their lot with outstanding courage. But courage cannot alter their place in society. Whatever the details of their existence, they are outcasts.

Chapter Five

Poverty Is Invisible

The two preceding chapters have discussed
the misery of the poor in the United States.
The Washington black ghetto has been used as
an illustrative example. Of course efforts have
been made by both public and private agencies
to help the poor. Yet it is obvious that these
efforts have not been wholly successful; for in
spite of them the poor continue to suffer. This
being the case, why is public opinion not more
aroused? Why are Americans not shocked into
very drastic action by the extreme agony in
their midst?

Blindness to Social Sin

There is usually a wide range of opinion on
the moral implications of any social problem.
Not only do Americans in general differ among
themselves, but Christians, including moral
theologians, share these differences. The abor-
tion controversy is a good example. Of course
everyone agrees on some propositions. No one
doubts that murder is evil. Yet even in such a
case there may be differences of opinion on the

appropriate course of action. Is capital punishment an appropriate remedy or is it not?

It is surprising and shocking that now and then practically every citizen will agree in supporting some national policy that is immoral. Even theologians and church leaders lend their support. It may be years, even generations, before people come to their senses and begin to realize the enormity of the error.

It is easy to give examples. Think of slavery. What happened in the United States is a particularly horrible example of a horrible system. Slaves were deprived of their most basic human rights. They could not worship God in the religion of their choice. They could not enter a legal marriage. They could not develop themselves mentally, for the typical slave law forbade teaching them to read and write. Moreover, a master could add his own special rules for his own slaves and enforce them by flogging or imprisonment. Yet this unspeakable immorality was generally accepted and approved, even by exemplary Christians.

During World War II, the United States and its allies bombed noncombatants mercilessly. They destroyed large areas of crowded cities, killing innocent women and children, the infirm and the aged. Such bombing was widespread and it is hard to estimate the entire death toll. However, it is conservatively reported that during the last year of the war, 135,000 were killed at Dresden and 84,000 at Tokyo. Then came the atomic bomb. Some 68,000 perished at Hiroshima and 38,000 at Nagasaki. The overwhelming evil of such mass murder should be clear. Vatican Council II was merely emphasizing the obvious when it called obliteration bombing "a crime against God and man himself." So was Pope Paul VI when he spoke of Hiroshima as an "infernal massacre." Yet the U.S. bishops unequivocally approved the war in their well-known statement of November 14, 1942, and they did not modify their stand during the bombing. Almost without exception Catholic moral theologians approved, at least by their silence.[1]

A final example will be taken from another country. The war that Hitler waged against the Allies, 1939–45, would seem to be a very clear example of an unjust war. Today probably no serious moralist would question this. Yet in his classic study of the subject Gordon Zahn examined in detail the numerous statements of the German bishops issued during the hostilities, and he could not find any question "or even a hint of any question" as to whether the war was just or unjust. When the war broke out the population of "Greater Germany" was es-

timated to be 40.3 percent Catholic, and therefore the bishops could have been very influen-
tial. Moreover, Zahn was able to find only
seven Catholic conscientious objectors who
openly refused military service. Of these, six
were executed and the seventh was placed in a
mental hospital. Zahn drily observes that each
of these received "no support whatever from his
spiritual leaders."[2]

Our American unawareness of the poverty
problem would seem to be one more instance of
this blindness to social sin. Of course we are
aware of individual instances of poverty and its
problems. Kind people form soup kitchens to
feed hungry men and women. Devoted religious run homes for dependent or deliquent
children. We have church bureaus staffed by
trained social workers who try to help in individual cases. But the problem is not individual
deviants; it is the mass agony described in the
two previous chapters. Recently the daily papers carried a story from Riobamba, Ecuador,
where a Latin American Bishops' Conference
was broken up at gunpoint by government
police. Sixteen bishops were ordered to leave
the country. It appears that the authorities
were suspicious that the bishops were critical of
government policies favorable to large landowners and neglectful of the poor. It will prob-

ably be a long time before anything like this happens in the United States.

Suppose you are in the company of some sincere, socially-minded Christians. Suppose you tell about the black Washington ghetto area where the death rate is three times the middle-class rate. Suppose you try to describe something of the agony of life in such a slum. People listen politely. They make some remarks. They raise a question or two. Then the conversation shifts to the next Redskins game or to a coming marriage or to the fact that a common friend has just bought a new house. No one turns pale with shock and terror at the thought of all those ghetto deaths. This is blindness to social sin.

Why Are We Blind?

One reason we are blind is surely the physical separation of the social classes. Middle-class people have no social contacts with ghetto people. People may develop casual acquaintances with a maid or janitor who works in their apartment building or in their office building. But the acquaintance remains casual. Moreover, maids and janitors are not typically ghetto people. They belong to the lower class of steady workers; most ghetto people are unemployed or only marginally employed. In sociological terms, maids and janitors are upper-lower class whereas ghetto people are lower-lower class.

The ghetto is physically separate from white-collar neighborhoods, although often the characteristic ghetto streets are only a block or two away from respectable, middle-class dwellings. The point is that middle-class people never have a reason for traveling that block or two. So in Washington they do not know those ghetto blocks: Ridge St. or Neal Pl. or Hanover Pl. or Kirby St. They never see those houses that need paint so badly. They never see the broken windows or the streets and sidewalks littered with broken glass, waste paper, cans, garbage, and other debris. So even near-by people do not know how the ghetto looks. And now the exodus from the city to the suburbs widens the gap still more. The ghetto is a whole world closed to middle-class people, both black and white. They do not know where and how the other half lives.

Anthropologists talk about "culture." They use this word to denote a special tradition, a distinctive body of beliefs and customs handed down from generation to generation. There is enough difference between the way dwellers in the Washington ghetto live and the way middle-class Washingtonians live to call the lifestyle of the former a separate culture, or at least a separate subvariety of the city's culture— a "subculture," if you will.[3] Certainly the differences are striking.

The distinctive ghetto dialect has already been discussed. There are many other big differences. Marriages are likely to be "consensual unions," that is, they are not legally sanctioned. Separation of man and wife is very common. The economy is different. Someone has spoken of "the irregular economy of poverty areas." This irregularity involves an overlap between the welfare and wage systems. It involves dead-end jobs. Often it involves earning money in illegal ways, for example, by "writing numbers." Attitudes toward police are different in the ghetto. So is health care. So are moral and religious codes. Even the food served at table is distinctive. Few middle-class people even know the meaning of "soul food."

Contacts between culturally different groups are likely to involve misunderstanding, and such misunderstanding often leads to injustice, although the latter may be unintended. The story of the treatment of the American Indian by white settlers on this continent is shot through with tragedy. The newcomers did not respect, or even understand, the Indian way of life. They expected the Indians to adopt the new, imported lifestyle which they considered obviously superior. What often happened was that the Indian culture was destroyed, but not replaced by the white culture. So Indians were left cultureless, confused, without a definite plan of life, and often very miserable.

Something like this has happened in the mutual relations between ghetto dwellers and the balance of the city's population. For one thing, the school system is designed to transmit middle-class culture. This aim is not attained in ghetto areas. Children there are too alien in their customs and attitudes to accept this new lifestyle that the school takes for granted. They drop out of school at the earliest legal age, quite unprepared to adapt themselves to our competitive economic system. So poverty becomes an integral part of the subculture of the Washington ghetto.

White-collar people are apt to regard ghetto people with contempt. The high crime and delinquency rates of ghetto areas and their implications were considered above, as well as the unfair judgments that these breed. But ghetto people also have their characteristic virtues that white-collar people are apt to overlook. My former colleague, Dr. Gladys Sellew, who lived in a slum area at Il Poverello House, used to say, "Middle-class people have pale virtues and pale vices. Ghetto people have striking virtues and striking vices." It is easy to see the contrast of vices. Murder and robbery are striking vices of the ghetto area. White-collar crime, like false advertising or infringement of patents, are pale by contrast.

But ghetto people also have striking virtues. Physical courage is one. Their life is cruel, but they face it without flinching. Children are not babied. Ghetto people are often generous with their meager possessions. A family is evicted, but neighbors give them temporary shelter. When food is scarce, it is likely to be shared. Ghetto people are willing to make sacrifices for one another. This is probably much less likely to be the case among the middle class.

There are two specific false judgments that white-collar people are likely to make about the poor. One is that the poor are lazy: Why do they just sit around idly instead of going out and getting jobs like the rest of us? The other judgment is that these idle folk live pleasantly on welfare, while you and I have to work hard and pay taxes to support their idle life. These judgments are absurd.

First, consider the judgment that ghetto people are lazy. This is contrary to fact. Unskilled jobs involve hard labor. The workers earn their wages by tiresome muscular effort.

In contrast, the white-collar employees earn their salary through experienced skill.

One mother in the IERP study separated from her husband and thus had the responsibility of supporting herself and her three children without his help. So she took two jobs as a hotel maid simultaneously. Every twenty-four hours she went to one hotel and did a full day's work; then she went to another hotel and did another full day's work. The double wage she thus earned was about equal to what a moderately good secretary would earn in a seven-hour day. Admittedly, this was an extreme case. However, it does illustrate the contrast between hard work and skill. Construction laborers sell their muscle; construction engineers sell their skill.

Everyday housework is harder for the ghetto housewife than for the lady in suburbia. Ghetto households have few of such modern conveniences as refrigerators with deep-freeze compartments, efficient vacuum cleaners, automatic dishwashers, clothes washers and dryers. Even the most ordinary equipment may be lacking. One IERP family had to wash their dishes in the bathtub. Frequently the gas or electricity was turned off, so that even the meager equipment the families had could not be used.

It is not easy to keep a wall clean if the paint is peeling or the plaster is falling. If a floor is made of soft wood and is chipping, it is not easy to keep that floor clean. If one does not have an automobile, carrying a bag or two of groceries from the store can be hard work. Money pays for conveniences and these conveniences save physical work. The poor do not have money.

Of course in this area, as in all others, there are great individual differences. Just as some men become so demoralized that they give up the search for regular employment, so some women find their housework too overwhelming to cope with. Yet it was much more typical for a woman to exert herself to the utmost in order to do a reasonably good job as a housekeeper. This was particularly hard for a woman to do if she was also employed outside the home. Yet success in fulfilling this double responsibility was found not to be rare in the ghetto.

Now consider the other accusation, that welfare recipients enjoy a lazy life at others' expense. Life on welfare is not pleasant. Welfare payments are scandalously small. As we mentioned, none of the welfare mothers in our IERP study had total family incomes more than about three-quarters of the poverty cut-off point. Living on welfare meant living in deep poverty. To choose deliberately to live such a life, one would have to be out of one's mind.

To live on welfare is to accept an inferior status. It means being officially classified as a failure. The social workers who supervise the lives of welfare recipients are typically kind and intelligent; but they must ask their clients personal questions to make sure that each one is legally eligible for relief. It is not pleasant to have one's personal affairs thus monitored by an outsider. It has been our experience that ghetto people are reluctant to apply for welfare. It is a last resort—and a very unpleasant one.

The Virtuous Who Do Not Help

It is a sad and ironic fact that many kind and charitable people become deeply involved in helping the needy who live thousands of miles away, while at the same time they seem quite unaware of the tragic poverty that exists within walking distance of their homes.

Cesar Chavez has aroused nationwide interest in the problems of the itinerant farm workers whom he represents. Many of my friends have become actively involved. They distribute literature, wear lapel buttons, boycott certain brands of food products, and even picket food stores that sell these brands. I even know of a local young man who went to California to work full time for the cause.

Certainly it is hard to quarrel with this enthusiasm. Chavez has a very convincing case. These farm laborers are without a doubt suffering from serious injustice. They need strong unions and now progress is certainly being made in the formation of such unions. It is not surprising that socially minded persons in Washington should be interested in such a serious problem in California. What does seem amazing, however, is that these same people should appear so utterly indifferent to the misery at their doorsteps.

There are many other examples. Mother Teresa has made a deep impression here and has aroused a great deal of interest in the work she does among the poor of Calcutta. A local church has a collection box with the sign, "All donations go to support Mother Teresa's work with the poor and dying." Within walking distance of this church there are tens of thousands of undernourished poor. Why is there so little active interest in them?

There is now a good deal of interest in the plight of Vietnamese refugees. I know a parish not far off that has adopted a Vietnamese family, and enthusiasm runs high. I know of people who have dug into their pockets and shown themselves extremely generous with individual refugees. Their striking charity is most admirable; yet it is hard to understand why the local poor are so neglected in the meantime.

The immediate reason for the apparent indifference of kind local people to the problem of local poverty is undoubtedly the lack of publicity. One hears little about the plight of the poor. A charismatic leader like Chavez can arouse national interest in the plight of the farm workers. A charismatic leader like Mother Teresa can arouse national interest in the poor of Calcutta. But the ghetto poor lack such publicity. Agitation by welfare recipients has been disappointingly low-keyed and unsuccessful. For a time the Black Panthers were promising. In spite of some violence, their primary thrust was a reasonable demand for justice. But the Black Panthers are no longer a force. We hear no shouts of protest from the ghetto. We hear scarcely a whisper. Ghetto people seem to accept their lot as hopeless.

Since there is no organized protest in the ghetto, there is practically no way for an outsider to help. Anyone at all who sympathizes with Cesar Chavez can immediately help in various ways. We can send a contribution. We can join a boycott. We can walk a picket line. But if we feel indignant at the plight of ghetto dwellers, what can we do? There is no obvious answer.

Perhaps there is another factor, subtle and unconscious, in our neglect of the nearby poor. Perhaps avoidance of guilt feelings plays a part. We can look with anger and contempt on the selfishness of the rich in Calcutta who let the poor starve. We can despise the selfish farmers in California who underpay their workers. But how about our own responsibilities for conditions here in the ghetto of our own city? Are we ourselves perhaps guilty? It is an unpleasant question. Better to think of the poor in Calcutta. We are not responsible for their condition. When we help them by giving to Mother Teresa, we are righting a wrong for which someone else, not ourselves, must bear the responsibility.

The Result

A consequence of the facts reviewed in this chapter is that Christian social thought often appears to be locked into a middle-class framework. Editors, educators, theologians, clergy, all seem to find it easier to understand the viewpoint of the dominant segment of society than the viewpoint of the ghetto poor. Jesus lived all his life not far above the subsistence level; few of us seem anxious to imitate this sort of life. One seldom hears an outraged priest preach a Sunday sermon on the misery of the poor. One seldom reads an editorial in a church newspaper along such lines. Our leaders seem to have developed a comfortable and friendly relationship with the powers that be.

Of course it is not true that U.S. Christians show no genuine concern for the poor. To state that would be most unjust. There are impressive lists of charitable agencies. Heroic people commit their entire lives to the service of the poor. However, the point here being urged is that all this charitable activity misses the central issue. It is not based on a realistic understanding of the fundamental nature of the poverty that exists in our black urban ghettos and in similar poverty areas. To explain and prove this statement is not simple. It will occupy the remaining chapters of this book.

Chapter Six

Christian Liberalism

The word "liberalism" is used in many different senses. Here it is understood as a program of social action that accepts the currently prevalent systems of capitalism and democracy and attempts to alleviate social problems within that framework. Liberals characteristically favor social legislation and strong labor unions to curb the excesses of capitalism, plus government programs of social insurance and assistance to the poor. Obviously, liberalism, as here defined, is inapplicable in totalitarian countries. Union agitation could not be expected to accomplish much within the U.S.S.R. However, liberalism can accomplish—and has accomplished—a great deal here in the United States. Specifically, liberals have helped a great deal with poverty in our urban ghettos.

Background

The history of the church's concern for the poor is long and complex. We have already spoken of this in Chapter Two. There is no need to attempt to recount this history here. However, two developments must be noted because they form the background from which the present system of Christian social action on poverty has emerged.

One development was the secularization, partial at least, of charity. This was a consequence of the gradual separation of church and state that tended to be total after the Reformation. This separation meant that the state accepted the ultimate responsibility for the care of the poor. The resources of the church were limited by the generosity of the faithful; but the state with its power of taxation was in a better position to raise funds. So today the existing immense welfare programs can be supported by the state, but they are obviously far too extensive to be supported by church people or any other private group. Of course the church is very active in the relief of poverty, but its programs tend to be specialized. They supplement the work of the state.

The other development was the Industrial Revolution. In England it began to dominate the economy during the last quarter of the eighteenth century; after Waterloo it gradually became dominant on the Continent as well. It involved the rise of the factory system and of capitalism in its modern form. The working class suffered from many abuses, long hours, low wages, labor of young children, for example. State intervention was obviously needed; but this was strenuously opposed by the dominant classes. It was argued that free competition would ultimately stop the abuses without special legislation. The fight for economic justice has been long and bitter. Even now much remains to be done.

In the light of these developments how can organized Christian social action operate? It can operate, and has actually been operating, along two lines which fall under the heading of Christian liberalism as here defined.

First, Christians can support progressive social legislation and they can bring to bear the special moral imperatives of their faith on such issues. For us, the oppression of the working classes is not only inexpedient; it is a social sin and we must hate it as we hate all sin. Earlier chapters have pointed out the supreme duty of helping the needy. Christians who take this precept seriously will try to mobilize the resources of the state to prevent poverty or at least to relieve it.

Second, it is clear that public welfare has by no means supplanted traditional Christian charitable programs. Often the two systems cooperate. Thus public funds pay for patient care in church hospitals, or for the upkeep of dependent children in church institutions. The use of public funds is defined and limited by law. Often aid must be withheld from a deserving person on account of some legal technicality. In such instances a non-governmental agency may be able to help. Then too, non-governmental agencies can experiment more freely than governmental agencies. They can try out new ideas.

These two types of Christian work for the poor, namely, political pressure and social work, will now be separately considered in the history of the U.S. Catholic church.

Catholic Social Protest

Before the middle of the nineteenth century U.S. Catholics did little to attack social problems. Catholics were an insignificant minority in the country's population. Their political clout was minimal. However, toward mid-century two developments radically altered the situation. First, a very large influx of immigrants began, and it included a rather high proportion of Catholics. Second, the effects of the Industrial Revolution, which were slow to reach this country, finally did begin to alter the economy, bringing characteristic problems. Thus, at the very time Catholics began to have political influence, they found themselves face to face with a new set of issues that called for new types of legislation.

During the second half of the nineteenth century the church's position on these social issues developed only gradually and was poorly coordinated. Most of the Catholic immigrants belonged to the lower working class; therefore one would expect a strong protest against the blatant injustices from which workers suffered in those days. The protest, however, was slow in coming. In 1874, for example, Archbishop Bayley of Baltimore warned against "the miserable associations called labor organizations." Such attitudes were often expressed. The turning point came in 1887 when Cardinal Gibbons succeeded in having Rome not renew its ban against Catholics joining the Knights of Labor, a strong and effective group. From this time on Catholics began to play an increasing role in the labor movement.

Excessive drinking was recognized as a significant factor in poverty. Thus the growing temperance movement had social significance.

The movement was strong among Catholics. A dramatic incident was the visit to the United States, 1849–51, of the Irish Capuchin, Father Theobald Mathew, whose eloquent preaching led perhaps half a million to take the pledge against drinking. On the other hand, Catholics, even in the South, did little against the obviously overwhelming evil of slavery. Indeed, when abolition finally became an issue, they dragged their feet. All in all, they were noticeably less active than their non-Catholic neighbors.

Perhaps, in the long run, the most important development during this period was the tentative effort here and there to discuss on a national level Catholic thought bearing on social problems. The Central Verein, founded in 1855, brought to America something of the social consciousness that had been developing among German Catholics. Then two national Catholic congresses, at Baltimore in 1889 and at Chicago in 1893, studied systematically the relation between Catholic doctrine and social reform. By the end of the century the social significance of theology was beginning to be recognized.

The later phases of Catholic social activism in the United States cannot be understood without taking into account their European background. The effects of the Industrial Revolution were evident in Europe earlier than here. It is then not surprising that social protest should become significant there before it became significant here.

The left-wing protest, which followed the Industrial Revolution, proved very significant. Count Henri de Saint-Simon (1760–1825) is generally considered the founder of socialism. He was comparatively conservative, advocating a sort of benevolent dictatorship of technicians and businessmen. The next stage is represented by four men, Fourier, Owen, Cabet, and Thompson, who proposed an ideal society consisting of small communities that would be largely independent and self-sustaining. The famous Brook Farm experiment in America was inspired by this European trend. In our own day the Catholic Worker group has tried out the same idea.

Finally, the protest became much more radical. Louis Blanc (1811–82) proposed social workshops to be supervised by the state, which would replace capitalism. Pierre-Joseph Proudhon (1809–65) held a labor theory of value. He would reduce the role of the state in his new economic order. Finally, the protest movement reached its climax with the work of Karl Marx (1818–83), who developed communism in its classic form. His theory is concretely exemplified in the various contemporary communist states whose economic and political characteristics are familiar.

It is not at all surprising to find that Catholic writers took part in this discussion of social justice. French writers were the most prominent. The golden age of Catholic social thought in that country was the period between the July Revolution of 1830 and the February Revolution of 1848. The chief concern of Catholic writers during that period was legislation to curb the excesses of capitalism. Of course this was liberalism in the sense defined in this chapter. Social legislation may seem routine to us. But to advocate it in those days was a sharp break with the widely accepted theory of *laissez-faire*. To break with this theory seemed shocking to many Catholics. These protesters included Olympe Philippe Gerbet (1798–1864), afterwards Bishop of Perpignan, Louis Veuillot (1813–83), a distinguished journalist, and Jean-Baptiste Lacordaire (1802–61), the great Dominican preacher. The greatest of all probably was the Vicomte de Villeneuve-Bargemont (1784–1850). He advocated a thorough system of social legislation. What added weight to his opinions was the fact that he was more than a mere theorist. He had held important public offices and his thought gradually developed from his experience.

Nineteenth-century Catholic social thought climaxed in the great encyclical *Rerum Novarum* (1891) of Pope Leo XIII. When this remarkable man was elected pope in 1878, he was already sixty-eight years old; yet he remained active and alert during the whole twenty-five years of his pontificate. He was decidedly an intellectual. A favorite recreation of his was writing Latin verse. His many encyclicals covered a wide range and were characteristically progressive. *Rerum Novarum* confirmed the position of advanced Catholic thinkers. Democracy is an approved form of government, although not the only legitimate one. Private property is a right, but not an unlimited right. It is limited by the duty of helping one's neighbor in need. Labor has a right to organize to combat exploitation.

One man, Msgr. John A. Ryan, played a surprisingly important part in the development of Catholic liberalism in the United States. Three things made his success possible. First, he was a trained moral theologian. Second, he was a very competent, though self-trained, economist. Third, he was a social activist with first-hand experience in handling social problems.

Ryan was born in Minnesota in 1869. He attended the seminary in St. Paul and was ordained in 1895. Then for four years he studied moral theology at Catholic University. His dissertation, *A Living Wage*, was widely read; the title itself reveals the direction of his interest. Then for thirteen years he taught at the seminary in St. Paul. However—and this is characteristic—he was very active outside the seminary. He attained prominence as a progressive. For example, he took an active part in pressing for minimum-wage legislation in several states.

In 1915 Ryan was invited back to Catholic University to teach. In Washington he was in a position to participate in some major national developments.

In 1919 he wrote the first draft of the "Bishops' Program of Social Reconstruction," and then he was appointed Director of the Social Action Department of the newly formed National Catholic Welfare Conference, a post he held until his death in 1945. The important post meant that Ryan was the official advisor of the U.S. bishops on social matters. Whenever the bishops took a stand on some public question, Ryan's influence was apparent.

Ryan's great contribution was that he interpreted and applied to U.S. conditions the Catholic liberalism that had developed in Europe. His teaching was along the lines of *Rerum Novarum*. In 1931, when Pius XI published his *Quadragesimo Anno*, it was looked upon as a further vindication of Ryan's views. His social thinking had been developing along the same lines that were expressed in this encyclical.

Ryan's fame and influence reached its apogee during the days of the New Deal. Roosevelt was conspicuously friendly toward him, and Ryan, in turn, was strong in his support of the president. Appropriately enough, F.L. Broderick's standard life of him is entitled *Right Reverend New Dealer: John A. Ryan.* The importance of this relationship was more than personal. Through Ryan and his relation to the government, Catholic thought gained a certain influence in shaping national legislation.

Ryan's enthusiasm for the New Deal was his strong point; but also, somewhat paradoxically, it was perhaps his greatest weakness. He seemed to equate the New Deal with Catholic social thought. The great encyclicals had emphasized both charity and justice; but Ryan seemed to read them selectively. His emphasis was always on social justice and he had little to say about the social implications of Christian love.

Msgr. Ryan's career has been considered here at some length, not only on account of the intrinsic importance of his thought and his leadership, but also because he typifies so well Catholic liberalism as it developed and as it has remained since his death. His followers, Bishop Haas, Father Cronin, Father McGowan, and his eventual successor, Msgr. Higgins, have been very faithful to his principles. So too has the hierarchy.

Of course there have been great developments since Ryan's day. The New Deal was succeeded by the Fair Deal, and then by the War on Poverty. But Catholic liberalism has remained supportive of such programs. Ryan was a strong advocate of equal opportunity for both sexes and all races. Thus he anticipated modern liberal trends. Ryan strongly supported our foreign policy, even when it led to war; his successors have done the same. It seems no exaggeration to say that Ryan's philosophy has remained dominant among Catholic liberals without serious alteration. Issues come and go, but they are still guided by his principles.

Catholics and Social Work

The history of Catholic activity in social work is quite parallel to the history of Catholic activity in social protest. Until the middle of the nineteenth century such activity was minor because the number of Catholics was small. But then the new wave of immigration increased their number; at the same time the Industrial Revolution increased the number of the poor, and the need for organized charity became acute.

There was a general trend toward organizing charity on a city-wide basis. It began in Buffalo in 1877 with the foundation of a Charity Organization Society, as such city-wide groups were called. Catholics followed the same trend. They began to organize on a diocesan basis. In 1898 the Catholic Home Bureau of New York began to handle child placement on a unified basis. In 1907, Baltimore became the first city to centralize the broader field of family social work. Organization gradually climbed to the national level. For Catholics, the significant date was 1910 when the National Conference of

Catholic Charities was founded in Washington.

Throughout these years, social work was gradually becoming a profession, and the need for formal professional education was obvious. In 1898 the New York COS organized a summer course. This became a full-year program, known as the New York School of Philanthropy, later the New York School of Social Work. Catholics followed the trend. In 1914 social-work instruction began at Loyola University in Chicago. In 1921 the National Catholic School of Social Service (NCSSS) was opened in Washington. This was a significant event on a national level because it developed directly out of the National Service School for Women, which was organized in 1918 and was sponsored by the National Catholic War Council as a nation-wide project to train Catholic women for work in connection with the armed services during the First World War.

This brief review of the history of Catholic social work in the United States can serve as a background for an even more important development. Social workers were trying to make their profession scientific. Thus something new was being added to the age-old tradition of Catholic charity. Msgr. William J. Kerby (1870–1936), whose influence was extremely important in this developing field, had this to say: "If it is possible to harm the poor by faulty methods of befriending them, the methods we do adopt may not be left to the whim of any one. They should represent our best wisdom. This means that charity must be scientific."[1]

So far, so good. But what, precisely, is "scientific" charity? The easiest way for me to try to answer this question is to call on my own experience. I was quite active in Catholic charities during the decade of Kerby's statement, having been Assistant Director of the Washington Catholic Charities for a time, having been active on a national level in conferences and surveys, and having taught at a social-work school, the NCSSS.

In a case of physical illness, it is easy to see why charity must involve science. One tries to make the best scientific medicine available to the sick poor. In those days we used to think that the behavioral disorders were more or less analogous to physical disorders. Diagnose the ailment, then it is easy to prescribe the appropriate remedy. It is perhaps significant that the social worker's most used text in those days was Mary Richmond's *Social Diagnosis*.

During that period, social-work education was much influenced by psychiatry. Dr. Thomas Verner Moore, the famous priest-psychiatrist, taught at the NCSSS and we all took his lectures very seriously. Psychiatry was the answer to disorders of behavior. Child-guidance clinics were very popular. At these clinics, psychiatrists, psychologists, and social workers would cooperate. For some years, I served as clinical psychologist at Moore's clinic. We psychologists would test a child's IQ, and the psychiatrist would take it as seriously as a physician takes a laboratory test for blood glucose. We felt we were on the threshold of a new era.

There was nothing inherently unreasonable in this attitude. Even one who strongly believes in the freedom of the will must admit that there are certain uniformities in human behavior. Given a similar background and a similar set of circumstances, most people are likely to respond in a more or less similar way. Then of course there are physical conditions that inhibit free will. Epilepsy, brain damage, even the normal processes of maturing and aging, affect an individual's conduct willy-nilly.

The real difficulty comes from the infinite complexity of human behavior. One factor in an individual's conduct is background. Backgrounds may indeed be similar, but they are never precisely identical, any more than the fingerprints of two individuals are ever precisely identical. And circumstances, too, show infinite variation. One may, indeed, often make a reasonable guess as to why individuals act as they do. But behavioral science does not go beyond common sense in the way that scientific medicine goes beyond folk medicine.

So, like many others, I became disillusioned. It is probably true that social work is now less confident of its scientific status than it was in the 1920s. Of course social workers can do a great deal. Specifically, they can do a great deal for the black ghetto and its problems. They can identify families eligible for relief and see that the relief is forthcoming. They can help someone get a job or a place to live. They can help a sick person get admitted to a hospital. But it is infinitely harder to make a delinquent boy give up his delinquency, to change an unstable family into a stable one, or even to cure a drug addict of the habit. Such triumphs do occur, but they do not occur in a regular and predictable fashion, as when a physician cures disease X by prescribing drug Y.

The Limits of Liberalism

It would be grossly unfair to minimize the good effects of the movement here called

Catholic liberalism. It has encouraged the passage of good social legislation. Most surely the problems of poverty have been assuaged by Social Security, by Medicare and Medicaid, by aid to the aged, to the blind, and to the permanently and totally disabled. Working conditions have been enormously improved over the last century. Benefits have been enormous.

And most certainly social work, including Catholic social work, has helped the poor in many ways. Large-scale government programs of welfare could not be administered without the regular aid of trained social workers. Without a doubt social workers have every right to be proud of their profession.

Yet liberalism has obviously failed to solve the central problem considered in this book, the agony of those 25 million poor in this most affluent land. Liberalism has indeed helped reduce the number of the poor; yet their number remains large to a ghastly degree.

There is another problem. Only a few of those who help the poor actually help them face to face. Most sincere and charitable Christians help only by writing checks. Those who thus help the poor at second hand are likely to remain ignorant of the real horrors of the black ghetto or of other poor areas. Because they lack first-hand knowledge they often lack any idea of the immensity and the seriousness of the problem.

Even among kind, intelligent, and well-educated Christians it is hard, for example, to find anyone who knows, even very approximately, the number of poor people living in his or her city. Few have any idea how high the death rate is in the ghetto. Most middle-class people comfortably assume that the poor are adequately taken care of by the various forms of relief without having any idea how cruelly low relief payments actually are. This ignorance is comfortable. What we don't know doesn't upset us. Liberalism lulls the conscience of the middle class.

Chapter Seven

Christian Radicalism

The term "Christian radicalism" is here defined—somewhat arbitrarily, it is true—as a system of activism which, instead of trying to reform the current politico-economic system, breaks with it entirely and tries to build a new society based on Christian principles. Christian radicals, as thus defined, are not revolutionaries. They do not try to destroy the present system. Rather, they hope that the new communities they establish will be so attractive that others will imitate them. The early Christians, they point out, did not revolt against the Roman Empire. But the pagans were so impressed that they were gradually converted. Christian radicals hope to convert the neopagans in the same way to the ideal of a Christian society dominated by love.

The Catholic Worker

Christian radicalism among Catholics made a striking debut here in the United States when the first issue of a new paper, *The Catholic*

Worker, was hawked in New York on May Day, 1933, to the amazement of the Communists and their sympathizers who had gathered in Union Square for their traditional annual celebration. The impression made by the paper quickly spread. The group that published it gained wide attention. Surprisingly fast, it grew from a few people operating from a tiny building on East Fifteenth Street to a national movement. The two people responsible for this development were Dorothy Day and Peter Maurin.

Dorothy Day, born in 1897, was the daughter of a journalist and became a very competent journalist herself. She was a convinced and dedicated radical and worked for such far left-wing papers as *The Masses* and *The New York Call*. Also, she was a deeply religious person. After early contacts with Protestantism, she was baptized a Catholic in 1927. However, she did not at first see how Catholicism and social radicalism could be fitted together. It was a problem for her.

Peter Maurin was twenty years older than Dorothy. He was born into a peasant family in southern France. Educated by the Christian Brothers, he himself joined the community and remained a member for about a decade. In those days the most radical group of French Catholic social activists was *Le Sillon*. For some time after leaving the Brothers, Peter was associated with this movement. Then followed a long period of wandering, first in his native France, then in Canada, and finally in the United States, during which period he worked at various jobs, on and off the land. Finally he arrived in New York.

It was George Shuster, then editor of *Commonweal*, who finally brought Dorothy Day and Peter Maurin together. Peter's brand of social Catholicism showed Dorothy how to connect her radicalism with her Catholic faith. U.S. Catholic radicalism was born out of the union of these two separate trends.

I first visited the Catholic Worker headquarters on East Fifteenth Street in 1934. What I saw had an overpowering effect on me. In my years of association with Catholic social activists and social workers, I had become used to well-furnished offices with receptionists, switchboards, bright and shining equipment. Or, if there was to be a meeting, it would be in a downtown hotel or perhaps in the airy auditorium of a local Catholic college. But East Fifteenth Street was different, very different. Those crowded, littered rooms where anyone could drop in, and many did, symbolized for me the contrast between those who accepted the establishment and those who rejected it. Later, as the headquarters was moved to other locations, the same spirit prevailed.

The physical atmosphere of the place was cheap and grimy; but the intellectual atmosphere was far otherwise. Indeed, it served as a meeting place for many of the most innovative Catholic intellectuals of the time. There one might meet Graham Carey, the acknowledged leader of the new Catholic art movement. His protégée, Ade Bethune, did many illustrations for the early issues of the paper. Dom Virgil Michel would drop in. He was the chief proponent of the new liturgical movement. He saw immediately the connection between the Mass and the new social Catholicism. After all, both centered on love. There were all-day discussions that would last well into the night. There new ideas were born, ideas that were destined to influence deeply the nascent Catholic ideologies that were developing in this country.

I found the words of the Catholic Worker people impressive because they were backed by their deeds, deeds involving sacrifice. They did not just talk about helping their neighbor in need. They actually did it. They did it in striking ways. They welcomed derelicts from the Bowery, those discouraged, helpless men and sometimes women. They sat at table and shared their food with them. When cast-off clothing was donated, staff and visitors shared them equally. Overnight the place was crowded with these visitors. All this seemed to me to be quite literally loving one's neighbor as oneself.

This Christian love of neighbor that I saw at the Catholic Worker seemed very beautiful to me. Was it not the very essence of the Christian life as described in the New Testament? I saw this same Christian love in Catholic Worker branches established in other cities. I saw it in the Friendship Houses in Harlem and elsewhere that flourished for some years under the tutelage of the Baroness de Hueck. I saw it in our Washington houses, to be described later. As a priest, I had intimate contact with many individuals involved in these action groups. I gave them retreats and days of recollection. In all my years of priestly experience I had never seen such spiritual beauty. Christian love has a transforming effect. Ordinary people can be lifted to what is really a new level of existence. To know such people is to be face to face with an astounding, unearthly beauty.

Christian Personalism

The spirit of the Catholic Worker was by no means a complete innovation. Rather, it was an adaptation to the U.S. scene of a new trend that had been developing in Catholic Europe. In 1938 I made a short trip to France to see first hand what was happening. I saw the work of the Jocistes, the priest-workers, and others. These groups used tactics very different from those of the Catholic Worker; but the underlying spirit was very similar.

The theoretical basis for this new sort of Catholic social action may best be described as *personalism*, specifically as presented in the works of Emmanuel Mounier.[1] Human beings are persons and this means that they are beings endowed with intellect and free will. Thus a person is able to examine a problem intelligently, think out a solution, and then freely choose a course of action that seems appropriate. Personalist action implies that one does just this. It implies forethought and a freely chosen policy. In a totalitarian state, citizens are not permitted to think for themselves. They are required to follow a path set for them by those in power. Even in a democracy citizens may follow the leaders of some faction thoughtlessly and automatically. Of course this is the antithesis of personalism.

Christian personalism may be practiced by an individual, even without the cooperation of others. Thus in time of war a citizen may decide for himself that his country's policy is immoral and declare himself a conscientious objector. A number of personalists may decide to act together as a group, but each freely makes the choice to do so. This is a striking feature of the Catholic Worker and similar groups. There is no coercion. For example, a majority of the members of a group may decide to support some strike and walk the picket line. However, if some decide not to support the strike, then they do not lose prestige.

It is thus an essential feature of Christian personalist action that it can be practiced by the individual, with or without group cooperation. What, then, can individuals do, working as individuals? They can apply two techniques. First, they can think through a social problem in the light of Christian principles. Having arrived at a conclusion, they can express it in public. If they have talent as writers or public speakers, they can do this on a large scale; but they are still personalists even if they communicate their belief only to their circle of personal acquaintances. This is the technique of *witness bearing*. Second, they can apply these principles in their own lives, thus helping to reconstruct the tiny segment of society where they have some influence. This is the technique of *nonparticipation*, a refusal to participate in what they see as social evil. These two techniques are illustrated by abundant examples in the New Testament.

Christ often described his own preaching and that of his followers as bearing witness. He thus describes his own mission: "I bear witness to myself and the Father who sent me bears witness to me" (John 8:18). After the Resurrection he passed this mission on to the apostles. "You shall be my witnesses in Jerusalem and in all Judea and Samaria and to the end of the earth" (Acts 1:8). The term is appropriate. Witnesses in court do not speak carelessly. They speak thoughtfully and convincingly because they are under oath and because they know that much may depend on their testimony. So, too, Christians must be convincing. The most convincing Christian witnesses are those who are willing to die for their faith. "Martyr" is simply the Greek word for "witness."

From apostolic times, Christians broke with the existing social order. They did not participate. Their lives were strikingly different. They did not scramble for wealth, but preferred to live simply and to share their goods with others. Their meetings were dominated by charisms and prayer. They rejected the conventional distinctions that stratified society. "There is neither Jew nor Greek, there is neither slave nor free, there is neither male nor female; for you are all one in Christ Jesus" (Gal. 3:28).

Limits of the Catholic Worker Movement

In 1934 and subsequently, many of us in the Department of Sociology at the Catholic University, both faculty and students, came to know the Catholic Worker rather well. We were all deeply impressed. The movement seemed to represent a giant step beyond Catholic liberalism. However, as time went on, we began to evaluate it as social scientists.

In one important respect the Catholic Worker went far beyond the liberals, who were swept off their feet by the government's officially generated enthusiasm during World War II. Even though the Selective Service Act provided for conscientious objectors, the Catholic hierarchy made no move to cooperate. It was

the Catholic Worker group that took the initia-
tive and provided Catholic COs with oppor-
tunities for alternative service in forestry camps
and elsewhere. All during the war the paper
provided a forum for anti-war criticism. The
entire present Catholic pacifist movement has
its roots in the Catholic Worker. This has probably been the group's proudest achievement.
However, this is beyond the scope of the present book, which focuses on a different problem:
the misery of the urban ghetto.

In some ways, however, the Catholic
Worker group merely reinforced the work of
the liberals. Thus their paper spoke strongly
and to a wide audience in favor of racial deseg-
regation and the rights of labor, often by means
of excellent on-the-spot reporting.

The chief day-by-day activity at Catholic
Worker houses has always been feeding the
derelicts, the outcasts, the homeless men and
women who wander about the city streets
without hope, often without any regular income or at best with a very inadequate income.
That the free meals thus provided constitute a
great act of Christian charity is beyond argument. It is a very necessary good work and one
that tends to be neglected by the standard social
agencies. However, by concentrating on a tiny

fraction of the poor, one may distract attention from the vastly greater number of the other poor.

The social outcasts who are fed in bread lines or in other similar ways do indeed constitute only a tiny fraction of the poor. It is difficult to estimate, for any large city, the actual number of those to be classified as social outcasts. It is hard to define this category precisely and still harder to count the actual number who should be thus classified. For Washington, perhaps Maurine Beasley's guess is as good as any. She gave an estimate of one thousand.[2] This is well under 1 percent of the city's poor as reported by the census.

By concentrating on a minuscule fraction of the poor, Catholic Worker groups tend to overlook the major problems of the slums as described in earlier chapters. Of course the aged poor, the sick poor, are also problems. Yet the chief problem of these areas is the problem of average residents, the normal boys and girls who find that local schools do not meet their needs, who drop out at the minimum legal age, functionally illiterate and untrained for any job. They may marry, but they usually find that normal family life is beyond their means. They are usually undernourished. They fall an easy prey to sickness. A few do, indeed, become the sort of outcasts that attract the love of Catholic Worker groups, but by that time their lives are wrecked. The great majority continue to suffer until they meet an early death, having been aided perhaps by our tragically inadequate welfare system, but probably not otherwise. By focusing on a tiny fraction of the poor, the Catholic Worker may even be doing the average slum dweller a disservice, as they distract attention from the less dramatic, but very tragic plight of the latter.

The social philosophy of the Catholic Worker looks toward an ideal society. As stated in the May 1977 issue of their paper, this will involve "a complete rejection of the present social order and a nonviolent revolution to establish an order more in accord with Christian values." It is disappointing to find that the ideal proposed is Distributism: "We favor the establishment of a Distributist economy wherein those who have a vocation to the land will work on the farms surrounding the village and those who have other vocations will work in the village itself. In this way we will have a decentralized economy which will dispense with the State as we know it and will be federationist in character as was society during certain periods that preceded the rise of national states."

A clear and quite obvious objection against this proposal is that it has been tried out rather often and has never worked. As stated in the preceding chapter, there was a wave of enthusiasm early in the last century for experiments of this sort, both in France and here in the United States. The Brook Farm experiment is perhaps the best known example. In spite of the commitment and enthusiasm of the participants, such ventures never succeeded.

It is surprising that Catholic Worker followers should still advocate Distributist communities after their own experience. Various groups among them have bought land in rural areas with these ideals in mind. Houses located on these farms have been pleasant places for rest, quiet work, and spiritual exercises. Yet they never developed in the direction indicated in the position paper quoted above.

One might even ask whether a society of the type described would be desirable, even if it were feasible. Is it really a good idea to turn back the clock? Do we really want to discard modern technology and restore life as it was before the machine age? Granted that many of the fruits of so-called "progress" are illusory, yet some of these fruits are good. Consider modern medicine, for example. It depends on an enormously intricate technology, the manufacture of drugs, the use of complicated equipment. It depends further on medical schools, on continuing research, on large medical libraries. Do we want to give up this complex technology for the sake of the simple life? In the United States the expectation of life at birth rose from 47.3 years in 1910 to 72.5 in 1975. Is Distributism worth the sacrifice of a quarter of a century of life?

The Washington Experiment

It was mentioned in Chapter Two that two members of the Department of Sociology of the Catholic University, Dr. Gladys Sellew and Dr. Mary Elizabeth Walsh, moved into the Washington ghetto and lived there with some of their graduate students, both black and white. Dr. Walsh remained for twenty years and the end result was the founding of Fides House, a large and formal settlement house. However, the most illuminating part of her sojourn was the ten-year period in a small row house on New Jersey Avenue. Her idea was simply to live there and be a good neighbor. Everything was very informal, but the informality yielded insight.

The Washington group was deeply influenced by the example of the Catholic Worker. It, too, was a break with conventional society, an attempt to identify with life in the ghetto. Moreover, it was spiritually motivated, very consciously so. Every day began with Mass and there were frequent days of recollection and retreats.

The Washington group, however, rejected the Catholic Worker policies in some important respects. The Catholic Worker had concentrated on only one of the problems of the slums, namely, the problem of the social outcasts, the derelicts, the 1 percent. The Washington group decided to concentrate on the remaining 99 percent. Meanwhile, another small Catholic group founded Martin de Porres House to serve the derelicts.

A second important difference was that the Washington group was built around a team of professional sociologists. It was felt that any plan to alleviate ghetto problems should be built on painstaking, factual, scientific study. So there was a constant flow of such studies, both by faculty members and by graduate students.

It is an important fact that these studies were made by people actually living in the ghetto; for it is hard to understand ghetto problems without actually living there and sharing, at least to some extent, the ghetto lifestyle. Dr. Walsh had been a professional social worker, but living on New Jersey Avenue was a new experience for her. Social workers visit the ghetto during working hours, but they do not know what life is like there at five o'clock in the morning or at midnight or on weekends. Social workers ask formal questions that are answered with circumspection, but they do not hear the day-by-day neighborhood gossip. Those who actually live there see ghetto life at its best and at its worst. Moreover, by living there, by being an actual part of the ghetto community, they develop a certain empathy.

The Fides House staff had different degrees of success with different problems. Probably their greatest success was with the young. One of the staff started an informal preschool. Another ran dress-making classes for the girls. Seminarians from the Servants of the Trinity organized athletic activities for the boys. The house was a place where, on cold winter evenings, boys could sit around, chat, and play quiet games. Merely giving youngsters something to do was helpful; it kept them out of delinquency.

It was harder to help adults. Their problems were deeper. Again and again crises would arise. Sometime Fides House could help. A family might appear early in the morning with the news that they were to be evicted that day. Then the staff would make a desperate effort to find the necessary cash to help them out of the emergency. Sometimes a job could be found for an unemployed man. Or a family might run out of food and apply to Fides House. A mother, eligible for welfare, might not know how to apply for it and a staff member could supply the necessary expertise.

After ten years on New Jersey Avenue, Fides House moved twice, first to a much larger single house, then to a very large building which had been a girls' academy. Both were provided by the Archdiocese. And a paid staff was gradually hired, although the bulk of the work was still done by volunteers. The result was a formally organized, head-on attack on the problems of the ghetto.

Along with this wider, more formal approach came more extensive insights. The staff came to see more clearly what they could do and what they could not do. They could do a great deal with the children. By keeping them busy and happy, it was possible to reduce juvenile delinquency. Then there were some successes with adults. The staff social worker might succeed in helping a family through some crisis. The staff nurse could help with medical problems. And there were successes with senior citizens.

All such successes were heart-warming. Yet gradually the staff began to realize that they were doing nothing, and could do nothing, to solve the essential problem of the ghetto. That problem was inherent in the very organization of the U.S. socio-economic system. Ghetto dwellers were excluded from any real participation in that system. Their voices were not heard. Few jobs were open to them, and those few jobs were menial, poorly paid, uninteresting, dead-end jobs. And without stable employment, stable family life is not possible. Ghetto people simply do not belong. Their needs are not taken seriously.

In the Fides House neighborhood a family usually undertook to support a child to the age of sixteen. It was difficult to do that much, and it was usually impossible to do more. At sixteen a boy or girl would drop out of school, this being the minimum age for doing so legally. At that time the child would probably be functionally illiterate and untrained for any job. It is extremely difficult for a poorly prepared boy or girl of this age to get any job in Washington. If one *is* lucky enough to get some sort of a job, it will surely be poorly paid.

There were many heart-rending cases. The bright, playful youngsters had made Fides House a joyful place. Then, after a few short years, they had become hopeless cases. One boy turned to robbery and spent ten years in prison. Another was murdered in a gambling dispute. Still another, after prison and a marriage break-up, killed his wife, her uncle, and himself on the street. Such cases dramatized for the staff the bitterness of ghetto life. And there was little Fides House could do. One might, indeed, hope to get a decent job for this or that boy or girl. This would be an individual triumph. But it would not alter the economic system with its built-in sector of unemployment. The ghetto would remain as it was.

Conclusion

Only one conclusion seems possible. Radicalism on the Catholic Worker model could indeed ease the pain of an individual needy neighbor. Personalism provided a most beautiful Christian lifestyle. But this, unfortunately, was not enough. It is not genuine Christian love if one helps some individuals and suffers an unjust social system to exist. For it is the system itself that makes our neighbors suffer. To tolerate the system is to tolerate their agony. Christian love is inconsistent with such toleration. To help one's neighbor in need requires a frontal attack on the evil system itself. There is no alternative.

Chapter Eight

Christian Revolutionism

Revolutionism implies the destruction of an existing power structure and the substitution of a different one. Revolution usually implies violence, but this need not necessarily be the case. In a democracy like the United States, an effective majority of the voters may simply oust the current set of office holders and replace them with others who will enforce a thoroughgoing revision of the socio-economic system. Thus a revolution may leave the political system unchanged while establishing a new socio-economic order.

Christian liberalism and radicalism developed in Europe and were imported into the United States. Christian revolutionism, as here understood, began to develop in Latin America scarcely more than a decade ago. As yet it has hardly begun to affect Christian leaders in this country. To understand the movement, therefore, we must turn to Latin American countries.

In the past many of us have been shocked at

the cozy relationship that seemed to exist in Latin America between the organized church and the selfish oligarchies that controlled the politics and economics of the region. Now a dramatic change is under way. Ecclesiastical sympathy is turning from the haves to the have-nots. In the meantime a new theology, called liberation theology, is developing to explain and justify the new attitude. Possibly the best way to understand all this is to examine, first, what is happening and, then, the theory behind it. The easiest way for me to do this is to recount some of my personal experiences.

The About-Face in Latin America

My first visit was in 1956 when I went to Bogotá, Colombia, to attend a meeting about the teaching of the social sciences on the university level (Primer Seminario Colombiano sobre la Enseñanza de las Ciencias Sociales en el Nivel Universitario). Being officially a guest of the government, I was invited to the homes of several middle-echelon public officials. Thus I could see something at first hand of the lifestyle of the group controlling the national policies. Practically all of them had been educated abroad, in France or Italy or the United States, and thus were fluent in a foreign language. The range of their cultural interests was extraordinary. They had unusual hobbies. A lawyer had just published a book of poetry. A housewife, whose hobby was cabinetmaking, with her own hands had made some beautiful pieces of furniture.

Yet this highly intelligent elite seemed totally unaware of the ever-present poverty in those acres and acres of shantytowns surrounding the city. But to a short-time visitor like myself, these same shantytowns seemed the most striking and conspicuous feature of the city. I met a group of young women from prominent families, including one of my former students, who were committed to agitate for economic justice in their country. They were discouraged. They told me they could get nowhere, for the simple reason that they could not make even the members of their own families see the great poverty around them. This was then difficult to believe, but it is no longer. I have realized that it is equally hard to make my U.S. friends see the misery of the ghettos so near them. Two decades ago Christians in Latin America were also blind to this nearby misery. As they are now changing, we also shall perhaps change—and for similar reasons.

In the past few years information has been gradually reaching this country about a radical change in the Latin American church's position on socio-economic problems. Probably the first important news concerned the Second General Conference of Latin American Bishops convened at Medellín, Colombia, in 1968. At this conference the bishops clearly denounced both "the system of liberal capitalism and the temptation of the Marxist system." They went on to state: "Both systems militate against the dignity of the human person. One takes for granted the primacy of capital, its power and its discriminatory utilization in the function of profit-making. The other, although it ideologically supports a kind of humanism, is more concerned with collective man, and in practice becomes a totalitarian concentration of state power."[1] Denunciations of communism by the hierarchy are familiar enough; but it was novel to hear this prestigious group condemn capitalism in the same breath.

Information from Latin America seemed so intriguing that I decided to make a trip and see what I could for myself. Therefore in the summer of 1974 I visited Mexico City, Bogotá, Lima, and Rio de Janeiro. In all the principal cities of Latin America, Jesuits have established centers for coordinating the various local efforts of Catholics to combat social problems. The usual name of such centers is CIAS (Centro de Investigación y Acción Social). Although these were established by Jesuits, the widest possible cooperation of others was sought. Jesuit friends here had given me letters of introduction to colleagues connected with the CIAS of each city I proposed to visit. This proved very helpful, and the whole trip was most instructive and informative. Here there is time to mention only a few highlights.

On my first Sunday in Mexico City I went to the nearest parish church and there I found a leaflet containing a list of suggested intercessory prayers to be used by celebrant and congregation after the Gospel. They were obviously not peculiar to this particular parish. Some of these prayers were extraordinary. The following is a sample in my own translation:

For the Holy Church, our mother, that she may not ally herself with the rich and powerful of this world.

For the capitalists, that, abandoning the egotistical pursuit of personal gain, they may put their capital at the service of the common good.

For the poor, that they may not desire to be able to exploit their brothers and sisters some day, but rather that they may desire better to ally themselves with them.

For the rich, that they may deliver themselves from the slavery that consists in being controlled by material goods and by the hunger to exploit.

For all of us participating in this Eucharist, that, recognizing the relativity of the goods of this world, we may learn how to relate ourselves properly to the goods of heaven.

The shantytowns found quite regularly on the outskirts of cities are sometimes called the "circles of misery" *(círculos de miseria)*. One of the most striking of those I visited was El Salvador on the outskirts of Lima.

El Salvador was an immense place. When I visited, it was only three years old, but already 23,000 families were living there. Eventually a total of 50,000 was expected. El Salvador differed in one important respect from most of the other such places I visited. Small lots were officially assigned by the government to families, whereas in most other similar places the people were simply squatters. Newly arrived families usually made themselves a hut with walls of woven reeds. Then they would gradually buy bricks or concrete blocks and build a more substantial dwelling place. Very gradually the government was building roads and installing water, electricity, and sewerage facilities. However, most houses lacked these at the time of my visit. There were many health problems. People would buy drinking water from trucks, store it in barrels, and drink it without boiling. There was much sickness.

Catholics were doing what they could to help the people of this immense, sprawling community. It constituted just one parish with a central church and five scattered auxiliary chapels. Several parochial schools had been opened. There was also a new maternity hospital, and a small beginning was being made with a vocational-training program. Local Catholics seemed anxious to help, but they could hardly be expected to keep pace with the explosive growth of the place.

El Salvador gives some hint of the depth of the misery of the Latin American poor. The unemployment rate there was about 65 percent, and yet 23,000 families had flocked there within three years. The misery from which they fled must have been even worse. And El Salvador is not an isolated example.

The measures that generous Catholics were taking at El Salvador were rather conventional:

churches, parochial schools, vocational education, a new hospital. This approach was not
that typified by the liberation theologians.

The approach was different in Tizapan, a
slum section of Mexico City. I found eight
Jesuits, two priests and six students, living
there. They were from a neighboring university. A sort of alley led from the street to their
dwelling place. It was very crowded; four of the
students shared one room. Conveniences were
at a minimum. This Jesuit community did not
attempt any pastoral or political work, for the
idea was simply to learn what slum life was like
by actually living there. Often the ideal life for
seminarians is thought to be one isolated from
the society about them, a life of study and
contemplation. But a priest has to deal with
social reality, either practically in pastoral work
or theoretically in his teaching. It seemed un-
likely that any of these students would ever
forget about the slums, after having lived there
themselves for some years.

Then I visited Ciudad Netzahualcóyotl, a
town some distance from Mexico City. This
had once been a squatter community, but years
had passed and the place looked like an ordinary town, not prosperous, but not deeply im-
poverished like El Salvador. The people were

poor, but not desperately poor. Here there was a community of four priests, three Jesuits and one Dominican. The striking point about the group was that they devoted themselves largely to political activism and political education. While I was there, neighborhood people began arriving, perhaps fifteen or twenty of them, for a class to be taught by the Dominican. The idea was to gather together a small group of neighbors to reflect on the injustices from which their class was suffering. Then they would begin to spread these ideas throughout the neighborhood. At his trial, Jesus Christ was accused of stirring up the people, which irritated the dominant elite of the time. These priests seemed to be trying to do the same thing.

One of the four priests, the Dominican, called himself a Christian Marxist. I did not have a chance to talk to him to find out what he meant by the term. However, many advanced Christian social thinkers in Latin America use the term and call themselves Marxists. This can be confusing. Probably most of us North Americans think of Marxists as those who admire the communist government of the U.S.S.R. and who sympathize with Russian efforts to foment revolution in other countries and to establish new governments sympathetic to Russia.

The Latin American Christians who call themselves Marxists are a different breed. Usually they are very unsympathetic with the government and the social system of the U.S.S.R. and its allies. They are Marxists only in the sense that they admire the work of Karl Marx as an economic analyst. Actually, Marx's analysis was quite acute. He wrote more than a century ago when business firms were predominantly small and he correctly predicted that they would gradually be absorbed by giant firms. He correctly predicted the enormous mechanization of industry. He was correct too in his prediction of the modern business cycle, a series of booms, each followed by a crash.

Marx also prophesied that capitalism would completely collapse. The system would destroy itself and leave the proletariat in control. This has not worked out quite as Marx said it would. Capitalism has managed to survive in most of the western world. However, even here there is something to be said for Marx. Capitalism has not completely destroyed itself, as he thought it would, but it has nevertheless experienced far more serious difficulties than the standard economists of a century ago expected.

It is hard to disagree with Christians who admire Marx as a critic of modern capitalism. To reject current capitalism, as it exists for example here in the United States, is by no means an unorthodox position for Christians. However, in the interest of clarity, it seems to me better to avoid the rather confusing term "Christian Marxist."

Even in the short time since my 1974 visit the news from Latin America indicates a widening gap between the dictatorial governments and the official church. Bishops and priests have been increasingly vocal in their denunciation of social injustice; and the power elites have reacted angrily. Dom Helder Camara, Archbishop of Olinda and Recife in Brazil, has been an outspoken advocate of the rights of the poor; but the government has forbidden newspapers to publish his speeches and writings and he has been banned from television.

In other cases, the reaction has been more violent. Priests have been shot or have mysteriously disappeared. In September 1976 the Most Rev. Adriano Hipolito, bishop of a poor suburb of Rio, was kidnapped, stripped, beaten, and left bound on a lonely road by terrorists. A month earlier, a Latin American bishops' conference at Riobamba, Ecuador, was broken up by soldiers armed with machine guns; the government had suspected that the bishops might have been discussing the prevalent economic injustice. At the present writing, thirty-three Jesuit priests in El Salvador have been threatened with death by a right-wing terrorist group if they do not immediately leave the country. Meanwhile, El Salvador Archbishop Oscar Romero denounced the "institutionalized sin" of "social, economic, and political injustice."

The size and importance of the progressive movement in Latin American church circles must not be exaggerated. There still exists some division of opinion. Conservative prelates, most conspicuously Archbishop Geraldo Sigaud of Diamantina in Brazil, continue to defend the old system. Yet the general trend is clear. The church is becoming increasingly united in opposition to the selfish political and economic oligarchies of Latin America. It is clearly emerging as the most serious threat to their power.

What has happened in Latin America is also

happening elsewhere. The church's newly active and dramatic struggle against social injustice is beginning to appear in widely scattered parts of the world. In the Philippines, in February 1977, a pastoral letter of protest was issued by sixty-six of the country's seventy-four Catholic bishops and read on a Sunday in the churches. It was prompted by the government's closure of some church radio stations and suspension of some church publications and by charges that 155 Catholic leaders were guilty of "rebellion and inciting to sedition." One bishop, the Most Rev. Francisco Claver, is already under house arrest.

In Rhodesia, Bishop Donal Lamont of Umtali refused to report to the authorities the presence of guerrillas who were fighting against the clearly unjust all-white minority government of the country. This could have been considered a capital offense under Rhodesian law. The bishop was arrested, tried, and sentenced to ten years in prison. However, the government finally decided to deport him lest in jail he be considered a martyr.

In South Africa the national hierarchy formally decided to integrate the nation's parochial schools in open defiance of the country's nation-wide segregation laws. Then the hierarchy went still further. They declared the integration of all churches, convents, and other church institutions. Black priests were to be assigned to white parishes. The church, furthermore, promised to boycott all businesses that practiced discrimination.

From all this it seems very clear that there is a new and worldwide trend within the church. Bishops, priests, and lay people are denouncing social, political, and economic injustice. They continue to do so in the face of exile, imprisonment, torture, and death. Indeed, the more intense the persecution, the more intense the protest becomes.

A Theology of Liberation

In recent decades there has been a good deal of talk about the "development" of "underdeveloped" countries. The process was often thought of in purely economic terms: the growth of the Gross National Product or of the per capita income of poorer countries. This attitude aroused some hope at first, in the 1950s. But people began to realize that development involved exploitation. Multinational corporations allied themselves with the oligarchies controlling the poorer countries.

Often the policy was to buy raw materials cheaply from the poorer countries and then sell back manufactured products very profitably. This was not of much help to the exploited masses.

In the 1960s disillusionment grew. Christian thinkers began to dislike what the term "development" represented and they began to talk of "liberation." The poorer countries needed to be liberated from the power of foreign corporations and the power of the domestic oligarchies. This would imply a social and political revolution that would bring about a thorough change in the living conditions of the underprivileged masses. This new viewpoint implied more than just a swing in political sentiment. Those who developed it saw it as an imperative of their Christian faith. They proceeded to put together a "theology of liberation."

The new theology is new in a very real sense. It implies a new methodology. Liberation theologians distinguish three periods in the history of their discipline. In the early centuries, the period of the Fathers, theology was a meditative reflection on the truths of revelation. Its aim was spiritual growth. Its great writers were personal and informal. A new school arose in the Middle Ages. This theology, best represented by St. Thomas, aimed at being scientific in the Aristotelian sense. It was systematized rational and spiritual knowledge. Now the liberation theologians talk of their discipline as a critical reflection on Christian praxis. The Christian life consists in a loving service of God and neighbor. Theology examines this love in its active manifestations and draws theological conclusions from this observation. "The pastoral activity of the Church does not flow as a conclusion from theological premises. Theology does not produce pastoral activity; rather it reflects upon it."[2]

Since liberation theology is so new, it is not surprising that it still lacks unanimity. It is still unstandardized. Various authors have their special viewpoints. These differences are not relevant here. What is important is the great emphasis all these writers place on Christian praxis. They reflect on it and try to discover its essence, the very core of the Christian life. They thus hope to help the church be ever more true to itself; they hope to be able to point out how to make Christian life more and more truly Christian.

Of course, to state that charity is the essence of the Christian life is not a new discovery. What is new can be expressed through the distinction between microcharity and macrocharity. The duty of helping an individual neighbor in need has been evident all along. Under the totalitarian Roman Empire, that was all the Christians could do. This is the sort of charity described in the New Testament. "Distribution was made to each as any had need" (Acts 4:35). That was microcharity.

But with the rise of popular power and the advent of democratic government, a new form of charity became possible, macrocharity, love directed toward whole oppressed masses. We have defined social sin as injustice, not toward an individual neighbor, but toward a whole social class. In a parallel way, one may speak of a sort of social love, macrocharity, which insists upon justice for a social class.

When Latin American theologians talk of liberation, they are obviously thinking of macrocharity, a Christian love that would seek to free the oppressed masses of their countries from domination by richer nations and by the allies of these nations, the domestic oligarchies. This is a love directed toward neighbors in need. But it is different from the traditional Christian charity that sets up agencies and institutions to help individual widows and orphans, the sick and the aged, and other needy persons.

The Christian duty to try to right existing wrongs is very clear; but it is not so clear how this is to be accomplished. The liberation theologians do not exclude the possibility of violent revolution, pointing to the Christian traditions justifying self-defense and the just war. Yet the Christian spirit demands using violence reluctantly, if at all, and only as a desperate last resort.

There are also practical reasons against cooperating in a violent revolution in the present-day Latin American countries. Fidel Castro did succeed in Cuba; but there seems little chance of repeating this success elsewhere. Camilo Torres, the priest who joined a guerrilla band of revolutionaries and died fighting in a Colombian jungle in 1966, has had great symbolic significance, but his death also illustrated dramatically the futility of armed revolution at the present time.

A further difficulty involved in revolution is that revolutionaries cannot always be trusted. History has many examples of revolutionaries who rallied the oppressed to their support and then, when they had attained power, showed themselves arbitrary and dictatorial. Communist revolutions have been typical of this. Thus it is dangerous for the church to endorse any revolutionary movement in Latin America. Post-revolutionary policies are hard to predict. The church might find itself allied with a power-elite scarcely better than the former oppressive oligarchy.

Under present conditions, nonviolent revolutions seem almost hopeless in Latin America, because most of the countries are controlled either by dictatorships or equally powerful oligarchies of the selfish rich. Liberation theologians have a vexing problem on their hands when they discuss how to accomplish their objectives. However, the problems of Latin America are not the focus of the present book. The question here is what can be done in the United States.

Liberation Theology and the United States

We have discussed the agony of the U.S. poor. Examples have been taken from the urban black ghettos, from the Washington ghetto, in particular. But of course the same agony exists in other poverty groups, the whites in Appalachia, the Chicanos, the American Indians, and other similar groups, totaling over 25 million tragic sufferers, the U.S. poor. So right here at home there exists a problem basically similar to the problem considered by the liberation theologians in Latin America, the problem of the oppression of the poor.

Admittedly, our problem is not altogether identical with Latin America's. Our nation as a whole is not being exploited by foreign capital in the sense that Latin America is being exploited. Nor is the political role of the church the same here. Nevertheless the essential problem is similar. Millions are being oppressed. This fact involves massive social sin. The church must become involved and this involvement must be oriented toward the basic social evils. Here, as in Latin America, Christians should reject an evil capitalism, just as we should reject an evil communism. Like the liberation theologians, we should commit ourselves to a basically new society, and this must involve basic social change, so basic that it could justly be called revolutionary.

So What Can We Do?

In the United States we have legal and constitutional means for bringing about radical reforms in our economic system.

Radical reform is perfectly possible in this country; but it is possible only at the price of extraordinary effort. A thorough change of attitude is necessary among the U.S. population. In our studies of the Washington ghetto, we uniformly found political apathy. There is little interest in social change. In the last presidential election, some 55 percent of eligible voters went to the polls, a strikingly low figure.

To work for social reform requires effort and sacrifice. Merely to grasp the issues, to see how specific causes lead to specific effects, calls for study, reflection, hard work. To advocate change calls for courage. The power elite do not suffer criticism lightly. They can use bribes, lobbying, sleazy tricks, and expensive publicity to discredit those who oppose them.

But to say that reform is difficult is not to say that it is impossible. There have been some minor triumphs here in the United States. A few of the worst abuses of capitalism have been eliminated by social legislation. And quite radical reforms have been brought about in some other countries.

The duty of fighting for radical, even revolutionary, social reforms does not cease to be a duty simply because it is difficult.

Chapter Nine

The Feasible Ideal

Too often economic reform has been thought of as simply a new compromise between capitalists and the proletariat. There is too much social unrest, and that is bad for business. So the capitalists make some concessions, better wages, shorter hours, more retirement benefits. In return, the wage earners will cease their agitation. The suffering poor will remain, of course, but they will remain an inarticulate minority. There will be enough social quiet for business to recover and grind on as before, and the rich will get richer.

This sort of political reform has been recurrent in the United States since New Deal days. It has resulted in much improvement; that is beyond dispute. Social Security, Medicare, equal voting rights, and equal employment opportunity have all promoted economic justice. Yet the poor still number over 25 million. As long as we tolerate this utter misery, we cannot be proud of our system. Change is urgently necessary.

Christian Love

A just society cannot be founded on compromise. It is not enough to yield just enough to our neighbors so that they will quit protesting and let us pursue our selfish aims in peace. The Christian's duty goes far beyond that. It goes extraordinarily far, as a matter of fact. St. Paul puts it this way: "The whole law is fulfilled in this one saying, 'You shall love your neighbor as yourself' " (Gal. 5:14). The implications of this command are remarkable.

If I actually love my neighbor as myself, I shall be precisely as much concerned about my neighbor's suffering as about my own. I don't like to be hungry or cold or sick. Under this command I must be equally upset if I find that a neighbor is hungry or cold or sick. And everybody is my neighbor. The Good Samaritan was a neighbor to the wounded Jew by the roadside even though Jews were very unfriendly to Samaritans. So, even if I think certain people are despicable, I must be concerned about their welfare. But this is not all. The New Testament goes far beyond that. I must be as much concerned about their welfare as about my own. I must love my neighbor *as myself!*

When we have a problem, it is not enough to

feel sorry for ourselves. Common sense demands that we think out a solution and apply that solution. Of course the same principle applies to a neighbor in need. We have to find a solution for our neighbor's problem. And we have the same duty toward the masses of the poor as we have toward the poor individual. We have a duty as Christians, an urgent duty, to seek solutions to the evils of society. Then, of course, we have an urgent duty to apply those solutions.

The saints, of course, furnish obvious examples of excellent Christian love. Many of them organized works of charity, often on a large scale, during their lives. Many founded religious communities devoted to good works. Those with power, nobles and high ecclesiastics, used this power to reform social conditions. Many, by their sermons and writings, aroused others to the duty of charity. The history of the saints is a history of loving service to the needy.

The saints regularly spent long hours in prayer. In the case of contemplatives, this is easy to understand. But why did busy executives, bishops of large dioceses or superiors of huge religious congregations subtract time from their administrative duties to spend it on their knees? The answer is, of course, that prayer, not clever administration, was the secret of their success.

The saints believed in the effectiveness of the sacraments, which are indeed strong social medicine. Penance is a rejection of all evil, including social evil. The Holy Eucharist is an affirmation of universal love.

The deepest characteristic of Christian charity is that one sees God in one's neighbor. To love a poor person is to love Jesus Christ. "Truly, I say to you, as you did it to one of the least of these my brethren, you did it to me" (Matt. 25:40). This is the secret of the intensity, as well as of the beauty, of charity. Love is the noblest of human emotions. Love reaches its climax when it is directed toward the all-perfect God. The key to the mystery of Christian charity is that it takes on this perfection, even when its object is some human being, superficially abject and wretched, but mysteriously sharing the infinite greatness of God—a fact visible to the eyes of faith.

This is the secret of the saints. All of us intellectually accept the fact that love of God and love of neighbor join to constitute the single and indivisible virtue of charity. The saints, however, not only accepted this doctrine in theory; they saw it with complete clarity. To them, it was an obvious fact that simply possessed them. To them, charity was everything.

It is therefore clear how a Christian must approach social problems. To support an economic system—no matter how superficially peaceful, no matter how superficially prosperous—that tolerates over 25 million suffering the agony of poverty, is simply unthinkable. To do so is to stand with that mob before Pilate and shout, "Crucify him! Crucify him!"

A fundamental principle of a good economic society must be the elimination of want. Private property is indeed a right, but it is a limited right. People must not be permitted to live in luxury while their neighbors lack adequate food or clothing or shelter or medical care. This is a most basic principle. It must be kept in mind constantly when we discuss the economic reform of our society.

Two Inadequate Alternatives

There are two policies, both widely accepted as possible future economic programs, but both very objectionable nevertheless. The bishops at Medellín saw this clearly. Liberal capitalism is one of these alternatives. It accepts the primacy of capital with its discriminatory scramble for profits. Communism, the other alternative, inevitably tends toward a totalitarian state.

For most of us Americans, it is probably easier to see the evils of communism than to see the evils of even a liberal capitalism. After all, we have grown up in a capitalistic economy and we take it for granted. We love the United States. We are proud of it. Under these circumstances it is not easy to face the fact that the U.S. economic system is fundamentally unjust.

The mere fact that such widespread poverty exists side by side with so much affluence should be enough to convince any fair-minded citizen that something is wrong. However, the real evil is fundamental. Economic injustice is not an accident. It springs from the very nature of capitalism. When profit governs the day-by-day decisions of business, the effect on the ordinary person will inevitably be considered secondary. Policy cannot be governed by the profit motive and by love of neighbor at the same time; for no one can serve two masters simultaneously. Under liberal capitalism the most that can be hoped for are a few compromises such as we now have in this country. These alleviate some misery; but those underfed and underprivileged millions are still among us, suffering.

Communism can bring about a wider distribution of income among the masses, but at an exceedingly high price. Intellectual dissent is stifled. People lose freedom of thought and speech. Russia is of course the oldest and largest example of communism in action. Wealthy capitalists do not exist there; but there does exist a privileged class of party officials whose standard of living is conspicuously higher than that of the masses. Nor is communism a great success in purely economic terms. Reliable statistics are hard to come by, but it is at least clear that after half a century of communism the per capita Gross National Product in Russia is less than half what it is in the United States.

A Middle Way?

A third possibility is conceivable. The means of production might be retained by private owners, but the workers, and the state itself, might become so involved in policy making that profit would cease to be the chief determinant of policy. It would be held in check by the recognized overwhelming importance of the public welfare. Owners would be encouraged to make a decent profit; but the elimination of poverty would be recognized as even more important.

Hardly anyone would question the desirability of such an egalitarian system as an abstract ideal. But is it practical? The overwhelming answer of traditional economists has been a very emphatic negative. Any movement in the direction of a welfare state, it was contended, inevitably slows economic growth. Even the liberal-minded have tended to be a bit cautious in pressing for reforms because they felt that these reforms would hurt the economy. Quite simply, they felt they were asking general sacrifice for the sake of an unfortunate minority.

Now the evidence is pointing in a different direction. Egalitarian policy need not hurt the economy. Actually, it tends to be helpful. As evidence accumulates, more and more economists are becoming convinced.

What Happened in Sweden

Perhaps Sweden furnishes the best example. When the Social Democrats came to power in 1932, social and economic inequalities were rampant. Then egalitarian policies were adopted and pushed consistently. Sweden quite frankly adopted the ideal of a welfare state. The results have been exciting. Unemployment in 1975 averaged 1.6 percent. There are no slums. Poverty has almost ceased to exist. But these happy results did not involve economic disaster. The precise contrary was the case. In 1975 Sweden's per capita Gross National Product was the highest in the world.

After the 1976 elections Olof Palme, a Social Democrat, was replaced by Thorbjörn Fäldin of the Center Party. Since the Social Democrats had been responsible for the country's characteristic social reforms, some foreign observers assumed that the election results implied a rejection of their policies. But the news since then has proved this view wrong. Sweden continues its egalitarianism. The shift was a change of leaders, not of policy.

Sweden's economic system is far too complex to be discussed here in any detail. However, a few particularly important features may be mentioned. First of all, taxes and charges for various forms of social insurance tend to be very high. In 1969 they totaled 40.4 percent of the Gross National Product, the highest percentage in any western nation. Moreover, between 1969 and 1974, total Swedish expenditures for social welfare programs (excluding manpower and housing-construction programs) rose, if allowance is made for the effects of inflation, by 45 percent.[1] Of course an effect of high taxation, including a steeply progressive income tax, is to discourage the amassing of large fortunes. There is little incentive to strive for an excessive income.

In many ways Swedish social welfare programs are similar to those of other advanced countries. They include such familiar features as unemployment insurance, health insurance, pensions for retirees, and help for the handicapped. However, these programs tend to give broader coverage and more generous payments in Sweden. Moreover, there are features that seem quite novel to Americans. When a child is born, the parents may take leave of absence from work with 90 percent pay, totaling seven months between them. The father may share this time and thus help care for the infant. Sick people receive a benefit equal to 90 percent of their normal wage. Hospitalization is free. A special "child allowance" is paid to parents of children under sixteen. For children over sixteen attending secondary school, there are also payments. University students receive generous study allowances, mostly in the form of loans, but partly as outright grants. Every worker has four weeks annual vacation. There are special programs to insure adequate housing for all. Day-care centers make it possible for mothers of young children to hold jobs.

In Sweden, as elsewhere, "social assistance" programs exist for indigent persons whose needs might not be otherwise met. However, the general programs of social insurance are so extensive that they take care of almost all needs; so social assistance or outright almsgiving totals to a small amount, less even, it is said, than most Swedish citizens themselves realize.

Certainly the most important aspect of Swedish egalitarianism is the way the economy is managed. This is not accomplished by state ownership of the means of production. In Sweden 90 percent of the manufacturing industry is privately owned and only 5 percent is owned by the government. The remaining 5 percent is controlled by cooperatives. Cooperatives loom large in agriculture where they are responsible for 80 to 90 percent of the meat, dairy, grain, and egg marketing. Consumer cooperatives have about a 20 percent share in retailing.

The secret of the Swedish system has been the voluntary cooperation of private owners, organized labor, and the state in managing economic policy. This cooperation involves an active policy that aims to assure "full, productive, and freely chosen employment" as a regular characteristic of the economy.

Some of the Swedish policies for reducing unemployment are familiar in other countries, such as unemployment insurance, vocational training, and job placement. Other measures are more novel. One example is furnished by the "removal grants," which help unemployed persons to move with their families to regions where more work is available. Also the central government has stand-by programs to place public orders selectively to help industries that are in trouble during recessions. Finally even though public ownership is quite small, proportionately, in Sweden, still this is available where it is actually necessary. For example, the state took over two shipyards in recent years because they were failing under private ownership.

So What Can We Do?

Let it be admitted frankly at the outset that it would not be feasible to improve the economy of this country by slavishly imitating Sweden. The United States is enormously larger. The total population of Sweden is not much larger than the population of New York City. And certainly the population of Sweden is very much more homogeneous. There is nothing there that approaches the striking ethnic diversity of the American people, a diversity that involves conflicting traditions, values, historical experiences. It would be enormously more difficult to agree on unified and cooperative economic policies here than it has been there.

Yet there is much we can learn from Sweden. Probably the most important single item is that egalitarianism is good for business. Those 25 million poor people here constitute an enormous drag on business. They are unproductive or underproductive. They have little money to spend in the economy. Though our welfare policies are cruelly inadequate, they are nevertheless a burden to the economy. Even if we forget the overwhelming Christian duty of helping the poor, still an enlightened egotism should dictate a radical change in our present system of profit-mad capitalism.

Though we should not try to imitate Sweden literally, the broad egalitarian principles of that country's economy can be accepted. Then, after a good deal of hard thought and experimentation, we should be able to work out ways and means for an egalitarian economic system that would be feasible under our special U.S. conditions.

There should be no great legal difficulty in doing this. A single law passed by Congress could, for example, radically revise our current income-tax system. If constitutional difficulties were raised against some radical reform, the Constitution itself could be amended. The big difficulty arises from the traditional attitudes of the American people. We are afraid of radical change.

As we have said, an enlightened selfishness teaches the values of egalitarian reforms. However, Christian love furnishes an enormously more valid and more powerful motive for change. It is a motive that rests on the very purpose of human life. We are here to love God and neighbor. This is our supreme calling. Indeed, it is our only calling, encompassing everything else. To fulfill our calling of Christian charity, it is not enough to give a dollar bill to a beggar or to send a check for a thousand dollars to the local charity campaign. We must commit ourselves—totally—to the reform of this selfish capitalistic economy. In a totally Christian sense we must be revolutionaries.

Chapter Ten

The Revolution Is Feasible

The program of Christian revolutionism appears frighteningly difficult. Well, why not? The New Testament makes it very clear indeed that being a Christian demands heroic sacrifice. But the goal deserves this effort.

The Cross

How did the idea ever get around that being a Christian involves only the observance of a few special rules, like going to church on Sunday, plus the usual obligations of the law-abiding citizen? Actually, the Gospels make it very clear that to be a Christian means a sharp break with conventional society and following a style of life that most of one's fellow citizens will find offensive.

Jesus Christ made it crystal clear. "He who does not take up his cross and follow me is not worthy of me" (Matt. 10:38). The force of this statement is blunted by the fact that we moderns look on the cross as a sacred religious symbol rather than as an instrument of capital

166

punishment. Perhaps we might try to translate it into modern language something like this: "You want to be my disciple? Good! Then follow me to the gallows. They tie your arms behind you. You stand there on the trap while the hangman adjusts the noose around your neck. Then they spring the trap and you are hanging there, choked and with your neck broken. Go through all that and you qualify as my disciple."

In a parallel passage, Luke 9:23, Jesus talks about taking up one's cross "daily." Literally, Jesus walked the way of the cross only once, on Good Friday morning; but in a broader sense his whole life, particularly his whole public life, was a journey to Calvary. His way of life and his teachings were a sharp condemnation of the establishment. When he denounced the rich, when he overturned the money changers' tables, when he ridiculed the pious scribes and Pharisees, he was stirring up opposition to the contemporary power structure. Every time he did such things, he was courting death, he was accepting the cross.

So the good Christian must follow Christ even if it involves the death penalty. The martyrs, who gave up life itself for the faith, were of course heroic. Yet they did only what every

Christian is obligated to do. Christianity is like that. Such are the obligations it imposes.

The program of Christian revolutionism is admittedly difficult. It means giving up the pursuit of wealth. It means breaking sharply and clearly with the unjust socio-economic system that now exists in the United States. It means renouncing the comfortable bourgeois life that so many of our friends are seeking in suburbia.

Alternatives

Suppose one rejects the cross as too difficult. What alternatives are there? The most common seems to be the pursuit of the success ideal. Get the right kind of education and then the right kind of job. Become upwardly mobile, as the sociologists say. Soon you will be able to buy a good house in suburbia. Perhaps you can start your own business. Then more success and a still better house. How satisfying to be a winner! What a thrill to be a millionaire!

On the other hand, financial success demands personal sacrifice. The *Washingtonian* magazine once ran a story, "How to Make a Million." Six Washington men who had succeeded were studied, and from their experiences certain rules for success were deduced. Here is one.

Spend as much time as possible with your business. Twelve hours a day, six days a week is the minimum. Days fourteen to eighteen hours long are average, and the seven-day work week is ideal. You will be forced to sacrifice family and social relationships until your business is solidly on its feet; then, and only then, you can begin to delegate responsibilities.

So there finally comes a time when the millionaire can delegate responsibilities, begin to take it easy, and enjoy his wealth. Or will that time ever come? Remember the rich fool in the twelfth chapter of Luke. Here was a man who was a huge success in agribusiness. In fact his crops were so abundant that there was no room to store all that grain in his barns. The solution was to pull down the old barns and build larger ones. And what a pleasant future to contemplate! "Soul, you have ample goods laid up for many years; take your ease, eat, drink, be merry." But it was not to be. "God said to him, 'Fool! This night your soul is required of you. And the things you have prepared, whose will they be?' " Of course not every rich man dies precisely at the peak of his success like the rich fool. But in any case the length of human life is limited.

"Eat, drink, be merry." Another alternative to the cross is a life of sensual pleasure. But this pleasure has a built-in limitation that makes it unacceptable as an ultimate ideal. When one pursues a sense pleasure too eagerly, it becomes self-defeating. It is legitimately pleasant to rest after a hard day's work; but too much rest equals sloth, which makes life ineffective. It is a joy to eat when one is hungry; but gluttony ruins health and shortens life. Christ and his apostles drank wine; but excessive drinking is ruinous. Family life is essential to society and family life involves sex; but unbridled sex ruins family life and brings tragedy to the individual. All in all, the selfish pursuit of pleasure is not satisfying.

Love

The noblest of all human abilities is the ability to love. The love of a mother for her children is beautiful to contemplate. It is unselfishness. She gives of herself, but paradoxically this giving of self glorifies her, makes her greater. Or consider the love of a man for his family. He does hard, uninteresting work, day after day, because he loves his wife and children and rejoices in supporting them.

A person's devotion to a great cause is a still higher form of love. To sacrifice oneself for the sake of social justice is sheer beauty. Here we encounter a paradox. The way of the cross is terrifying and repulsive. Yet at the same time the way of the cross is beautiful. It is the supreme act of love and great love is great self-fulfillment.

The most terrifying fact that we all must face is death. The fruits of conventional success —money, power—are unable to help us avoid this terrifying destiny. But love? "Love is strong as death" (Song of Sol. 8:6).

To create a morally just society here on earth does indeed involve sacrifice. It means the renunciation of the conventional success ideal. It means loving one's most unattractive neighbors and sharing what one has with them. So in a sense it is the way of the cross. Yet, strange to say, in another sense it is a foretaste of heaven. It is a life of fiery love of God in our neighbor.

There is a certain parallel between the life of an individual and the life of a society. Selfish individuals are unlovely. Their lives are not beautiful. They are evil and evil cannot be satisfying. So also the selfish, competitive society.

In such a society the poor suffer while the rich enjoy only a pathological sort of pleasure. But the virtuous society is a happy place. Because citizens are ready to share their goods, there is no one in want. And this sharing is a holy joy.

Hate

Just as people reach their moral apogee through love, so they reach their moral nadir through hate. Hate is the rejection of God and neighbor. It need not be a strong emotion. The wicked in the twenty-fifth chapter of Matthew merely neglected their needy neighbors. They left them hungry, shivering, and homeless. This was hatred without emotion. But it is deadly.

The social sin that most horrifies us in modern times is probably the Nazi slaughter of the European Jews. It seems utterly diabolical that Jews should be systematically rounded up, brought to concentration camps, and slaughtered. We shudder when we realize that human nature can sink so low. Yet is there not a certain parallel between the camps and our American ghettos? The Germans herded Jews into death camps; we herd the black poor into death neighborhoods. It is true that the Jews were killed off much faster. But their systematic slaughter was a temporary insanity. It lasted only from 1941 to the fall of Germany in 1945. On the other hand, the death neighborhoods where we kill the blacks are a permanent feature of our society. It takes us a year to kill off an extra 200 by neglect in the tiny Service Area 6, Sub-Area B. They could kill that many in a few hours at Auschwitz or Treblinka. In our ghettos we slaughter by neglect. In the camps they slaughtered by lethal gas. Yet is that really an essential difference?

The Nazis killed by postive action; we kill by neglect. We kill as the damned did in the twenty-fifth chapter of Matthew. These did not go out of their way to injure their needy neighbors. They simply neglected them.

Notes

Chapter 1

1. See Paul Hanly Furfey, *"Plousios* and Cognates in the New Testament," *Catholic Biblical Quarterly*, July 1943. This article discusses also the general economic situation in classical times and the personal characteristics of the wealthy in those days.

Chapter 2

1. See particularly Mary Elizabeth Walsh, *The Saints and Social Work* (Silver Spring, Maryland: Preservation of the Faith, 1937). The author studies the lives of all the beatified persons and canonized saints, except the martyrs who lived within the century before the book was written, and compares their treatment of the poor with that advocated by modern social work.

Chapter 3

1. Figures from Department of State, *Background Notes on the Countries of the World*, various issues, January 1974 to June 1976.

2. Evelyn M. Kitagawa and Philip M. Hauser, *Differential Mortality in the United*

States: A Study in Socioeconomic Epidemiology (Cambridge: Harvard University Press, 1973), pp. 178–79.

3. Ibid., p. 151.

Chapter 4

1. George N. Putnam and Edna M. O'Hern, "The Status Significance of an Isolated Urban Dialect," Supplement to *Language*, October-December 1955.

Chapter 5

1. As far as I can determine, only two U.S. Catholic priests publicly disapproved the bombing in written statements during the war. See John C. Ford, "The Morality of Obliteration Bombing," *Theological Studies* 5 (1944), pp. 261–309; and Paul Hanly Furfey, "Bombing of Noncombatants Is Murder," *The Catholic C.O.* (July-September 1945), pp. 3–4, and the same author's *The Mystery of Iniquity* (Milwaukee: Bruce, 1944), pp. 165–66.

2. Gordon C. Zahn, *German Catholics and Hitler's Wars* (New York: Sheed and Ward, 1962), pp. 68, 54, 9.

3. See P.H. Furfey, *The Subculture of the Washington Ghetto* (Washington, D.C.: Bureau of Social Research, Catholic University of America, 1972).

Chapter 6

1. *The Social Mission of Charity* (New York: Macmillan, 1924), p. 7.

Chapter 7

1. See particularly his book *Révolution personnaliste et communautaire* (Paris: Aubier, 1935).

2. In Veronica Maz, *The Stick-Carrier* (Hicksville, N.Y.: Exposition Press, 1975), p. 15.

Chapter 8

1. Second General Conference of Latin American Bishops, *The Church in the Present-Day Transformation of Latin America in the Light of the Council*, vol. 2: *Conclusions* (Washington, D.C.: United States Catholic Conference, Division for Latin America, 1973), p. 45.

2. Gustavo Gutiérrez, *A Theology of Liberation*, trans. and ed. Caridad Inda and John Eagleson (Maryknoll, N.Y.: Orbis, 1973), p. 11.

Chapter 9

1. Leif Holgersson and Stig Lundström, *The Evolution of Swedish Social Welfare* (Nyköping: The Swedish Institute, 1975), pp. 39–40.